Secrets &
Mysteries
OF THE WORLD

Also by Sylvia Browne

<u>Audio/CD Programs</u>
Angels and Spirit Guides
Angels, Guides & Ghosts
Healing Your Body, Mind, and Soul
Life on the Other Side (audio book)
Making Contact with the Other Side
Meditations
The Other Side of Life
Prayers
Secrets & Mysteries of the World (audio book)
Sylvia Browne's Book of Angels
Sylvia Browne's Tools for Life
and . . .
The Sylvia Browne Newsletter (bimonthly)

All of the above are available
at your local bookstore, or may be ordered by visiting:
Hay House USA: **www.hayhouse.com**
Hay House Australia: **www.hayhouse.com.au**
Hay House UK: **www.hayhouse.co.uk**
Hay House South Africa: **orders@psdprom.co.za**

Secrets & Mysteries
OF THE WORLD

Sylvia Browne

HAY HOUSE, INC.
Carlsbad, California
London • Sydney • Johannesburg
Vancouver • Hong Kong

Published and distributed in the United States by: Hay House, Inc., P.O. Box 5100, Carlsbad, CA 92018-5100 • *Phone:* (760) 431-7695 or (800) 654-5126 • *Fax:* (760) 431-6948 or (800) 650-5115 • www.hayhouse.com • *Published and distributed in Australia by:* Hay House Australia Pty. Ltd., 18/36 Ralph St., Alexandria NSW 2015 • *Phone:* 612-9669-4299 • *Fax:* 612-9669-4144 • www.hayhouse.com.au • *Published and distributed in the United Kingdom by:* Hay House UK, Ltd. • Unit 62, Canalot Studios • 222 Kensal Rd., London W10 5BN • *Phone:* 44-20-8962-1230 • *Fax:* 44-20-8962-1239 • www.hayhouse.co.uk • *Published and distributed in the Republic of South Africa by:* Hay House SA (Pty), Ltd., P.O. Box 990, Witkoppen 2068 • *Phone/Fax:* 2711-7012233 • orders@psdprom.co.za • *Distributed in Canada by:* Raincoast • 9050 Shaughnessy St., Vancouver, B.C. V6P 6E5 • *Phone:* (604) 323-7100 • *Fax:* (604) 323-2600

Editorial supervision: Jill Kramer • *Design:* Amy Rose Szalkiewicz
Interior illustrations: Kirk Simonds

Sylvia would like to thank all the contributors who granted permission to reproduce their photographs in this book: Special thanks to Sylvia's friends Nick and Khrys Nocerino for allowing photos to be taken of ShaNaRa. Nick Nocerino's research in the field of crystal skulls is unparalleled. Thanks also to Kirby Seid. *Crystal Skull photos:* © Sylvia Browne Corp. / *Piri Ries Map:* © David Hatcher Childress, Adventures Unlimited Press: www.wexclub.com / UFO and *crop-circle photos:* © Colin Andrews: www.CropCircleInfo.com / *Shroud of Turin photo:* © Barrie Schwartz: www.shroud.com / *Nazca Plain photos:* © www.anthroarcheart.org

Library of Congress Cataloging-in-Publication Data

Browne, Sylvia.
    Secrets & mysteries of the world / Sylvia Browne.
        p. cm.
    ISBN 1-4019-0085-2 — ISBN 1-4019-0458-0 1. Occultism. 2. Parapsychology.
I. Title:
Secrets and mysteries of the world. II. Title.
    BF1411.B78 2005
    133.9'1—dc22
        2003026565

Hardcover ISBN 1-4019-0085-2
Tradepaper ISBN 1-4019-0458-0

08 07 06 05   5 4 3 2
1st printing, January 2005
2nd printing, January 2005

Printed in the United States of America

To Dal Brown, for his help and support

Contents

Introduction

In this book, you'll read about some of the secrets and mysteries that have greatly puzzled humankind, in some cases for centuries. Naturally, I've always been fascinated with the unexplained—I don't think I need to go into every nuance of how I've spent years researching and studying the phenomena that you're going to read about in these pages. Those of you who aren't aware, take my word for it: Yes, I'm a spiritual psychic and a student of theology, but my interest in the world's secrets and ancient myths, as well as the afterlife, has been a continual and ongoing passion.

You may not agree with my arguments or research, and that's fine . . . just stay with me and see if more often than not, the time, the place, the historical implications, or the plain logic will bear out the truth of what I say. My psychic abilities also come heavily into play here to augment the intense research I've done, but as I've always said, "Take with you what you want and leave the rest."

I've personally visited most of the places where the mysteries in this book originate. I've walked the paths and used myself as a psychic barometer first, and then I've gone back to see if I could prove what I telepathically picked up using research, statistics, eyewitness accounts, and sometimes just good ol' common sense. Many times, as you'll see, I've gone on a mystery hunt with tongue firmly planted in cheek, only to be knocked sideways with proof; while other times a "sure thing" turned out to be *too* shrouded in myth—it was too unlikely, or there wasn't enough evidence—and I was too disappointed to put my stamp of approval on it.

The reason this book has been written at all was greatly due to Reid Tracy, president of Hay House (the publisher of this work). We were sitting over lunch one day, and I was regaling him with stories from Egypt and other locales I've visited. Finally, he looked up at me and asked, "Why don't you write about all these places you've been to and come up with your take on them?"

I chewed it over for a while as I wondered if there were any books I'd read that covered all the places and things I've seen. There's Erich Von Daniken's *Chariots of the Gods: Unsolved Mysteries of the Past*, but that just deals with UFOs; and besides, his book was so controversial when it was first published that scientists came out of the woodwork in hordes to debunk it. I then realized that of all the "research" books I've read (and there have been many), they all have one thing in common: their detractors. I mean, I wouldn't be writing this book if these mysteries had ever been fully explained—that's

INTRODUCTION

what makes them mysteries. Of course I know that there will be those skeptics who'll say that this book is all hogwash, but you'll see as you read through the following chapters how fascinating some of the twists and turns have been. . . .

I have to stop here and explain that even though I've never written a book like this before, please don't feel that I've taken leave of my senses. Some of what I'm about to say I can't prove, but as we get into more of the stories, you'll see how many well-known archaeologists, historians, and anthropologists have backed up my psychic insights. People such as famed paleoanthropologist and conservationist Dr. Richard Leakey; Dr. Zahi Hawass, Secretary General of the Supreme Council of Antiquities in Egypt; and others who tend to trust me are not given to flights of fancy.

Now, this work isn't meant to be a scientific treatise. Instead, I've written it with the average reader in mind, who may know little or nothing about the mysteries herein. Although my own research contains scientific sources, I'm sure that I've missed some. Keep in mind that this book is meant to give an overview of the secrets and mysteries of the world and then offer my psychic interpretations of them. Sure, my field of endeavor is nothing if not controversial, but you know me: I jump in where angels fear to tread.

As you read, I hope that you'll gain insight and hope—but if nothing else, you'll at least take away a feeling of action as you either agree or disagree with what I'm presenting here. When you start searching, you'll be a Gnostic (a seeker of truth) of sorts, because as Jesus said, "Seek and ye shall find, knock and it shall be opened unto you." After all, the search for truth makes us see through all the confusion and get down to brass tacks.

Read everything with an open mind and with discernment, and don't believe something just because I (or someone else) say it's true . . . you will and should find your own divine truth, which is yours alone.

Get ready for your journey—and this time buckle up, because you're in for one heck of a ride.

Part I

Mysterious Places

I

Stonehenge

On the Salisbury Plain in England lies a magnificent stone circle that was once used for religious ceremonies and has been attributed to the Druids, a caste of Celtic priests. Although they may have used it, its beginnings actually go back to the Neolithic people of the British Isles.

Some historians say that Stonehenge dates to about 3000 B.C., but I felt when I was there that it was more like 5000 B.C. And while the circle has been rebuilt many times, it has somehow managed to keep the same general configurations.

There are more than a thousand stone circles in the British Isles, but nothing is as remarkable as Stonehenge. It's the only one consisting of 30 upright stones (17 of which still stand) that were chiseled, smoothed, and imported from outside the local area, and it's the only one with lintel stones that were shaped into curves and placed on top of the upright stones, forming a circle of doorways.

It's interesting to note that the axis of Stonehenge, which divides the circle and aligns with its entrance, is oriented toward the midsummer solstice sunrise; while in nearby Ireland, the monument Newgrange, which was built at approximately the same time, is directed toward the midwinter solstice sunrise. Now, we can surmise that this was some kind of calendar—and I'm sure that this was a small part of it because humans have always been interested in the heavens—but as we'll see, the placement of the stones had a deeper spiritual meaning. It's as if they carried a vibration of protective energy to keep negativity out and give the people inside safety and grace.

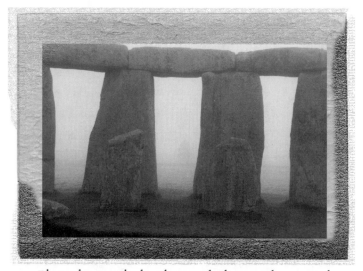

Photo showing the lintel stones laid across the top circle
of stones at Stonehenge.

Stonehenge has come to be studied by *archaeoastronomists*, who track the astronomical practices of ancient cultures. You see, even in primitive or ancient times, people such as the Egyptians (who will be addressed later) were extremely interested in the phases of the sun and moon and the configuration of the stars.

I'm sure that they used the seasons for planting; or anticipating rainfalls, temperature changes, or floods, paying particular attention to the phases of the moon. (Even in today's world, you have only to ask anyone in emergency rooms, police departments, or my own profession what kind of bizarre things come about during a full moon. Doctors have studied women's menstrual flows along with the cycles of the moon for years—after all, it makes sense that if the oceans are affected, why not our physical well-being? And *The Old Farmer's Almanac* is based not only on seasons, but also on what phase the moon is in during these times. So none of this is without some basis in fact and research.)

While there's no doubt that Stonehenge did have a definite astrophysical implication, I feel that many researchers have missed the greater spiritual insights inherent in its existence.

Piercing the Veil at Stonehenge

When I first visited Stonehenge in 1978, there were no barriers, so you could freely roam over and around the stones. I recently returned with a group of people, and I was again allowed to examine the stones and get all the vibrations I needed. The ability to touch an object and psychically access its history through energy is called *psychometry.* Since everything in nature carries an imprint, you only have to be able to tap in to it, and the whole story will unfold. Like many other places we'll explore in this book, the rocks of Stonehenge contain the vibrations of layers upon layers of different times, peoples, and rituals that I was able to pick up on.

The first types of feedback I began to get were images of people—hundreds of individuals dragging huge monoliths across a plain. The rocks seemed to have been cut and mined from an ancient quarry in southwest England. There were also giant pulleys on a crudely constructed, yet fairly sophisticated, machine, with wheels and rope that hoisted the stones up. The men pulling the stones were very primitive looking, wearing animal skins and hats and sporting facial tattoos. In a time-altering, fast-forward sort of way, I could see them putting the stones in a circle. They also seemed to have some type of rope that measured the distances. I could hear them shouting and grunting, but in a language that sounded like nothing I've ever heard.

On the outside of this perfect stone circle, there was a group of women and children sitting or standing and watching with rapt attention. Every once in a while, a jubilant exclamation would come out of some of the women's mouths, as if to cheer the men on. I noticed that the women and children seemed to be fingering red beads or berries that were strung together. It reminded me of Catholics saying the rosary for a special miracle or prayer.

After the monoliths were in place, they looked shiny and white—certainly not like the gray color they are now. When the circle was finished, everyone came into it and knelt, not in a supplicant manner, but as if this was the right and comfortable posture. The circle seemed to be a haven for them, keeping negativity outside. (Think about how many times we surround ourselves with the White Light of the Holy Spirit—who's to say that these stones might not have served as protection from random hordes of marauding bands?) It seemed that for whatever reason, these people felt that while they were in the circle, their god (or gods) protected them.

Next, a very tall man appeared, dressed in a bright red cape and a tall, cone-shaped hat with starlike points coming out of it. He began to go in and out of the stone doorways—and each time

he did, he would take off his cape; when he got through the doorway, he'd put it back on.

It looked to me like he was showing rebirth: going through the portal of life with nothing, and then assuming the posture of putting on earthly garb. The man then began a charade. He pointed to a woman and instructed her to pick up a baby and stand with him, thus signifying the continuation of the lineage.

The group began uttering a guttural-sounding chant; then, as if from nowhere, fruits, vegetables, and some kind of nut were served. The tall, caped man looked around at the circle and seemed to be pleased. Then his eyes moved over the crowd and settled on a dark, unshaven male huddled in a type of animal cloak. He pointed his finger at the smaller man and made what sounded like a clucking noise, and the crowd joined in. He beckoned the man toward him, who approached with head bent. The tall man held out his hand, and the shorter, shabby male dropped two golden objects into his palm. The man with the cape then turned to a woman behind him and gave her the objects. She seemed surprised and relieved, grabbed them, and humbly knelt down.

The tall man pointed for the other male to leave the circle, yet he seemed to beg not to be banished. I thought, *He's a thief and is being sent away.* As soon as I thought this, the short man resolutely limped out of the circle and soon vanished into the fog that was beginning to envelop the plains. I was recording everything on tape at the time and said, "Well, justice was meted out here for thieves and those who broke the law." I knew this was a very primitive time, but I still felt that these people had a social structure as well as a moral conscience. They didn't appear strange except for their clothing (or lack thereof); in fact, in their own way, they seemed cared for and certainly didn't look undernourished.

Then the scene changed. I don't know exactly how to describe how this happens, but it's like watching a movie—it's almost as if I'm in a mental time machine, and when it starts, it just continues until I want to stop it. I now noticed what I hadn't seen before: a huge white stone right in the center of the circle. The caped figure would point to each man, who would then come up and place a very primitive spear on the altarlike rock, which seemed to have the power to give the men courage and lend strength to their weapons.

The Most Magnificent of Burial Grounds

Around A.D. 1135, Geoffrey of Monmouth, in his work *The History of the Kings of Briton,* claimed that Stonehenge was brought from Africa to Ireland by a tribe of giants; from there, it was flown by the magician Merlin across the sea to its present site. It seems that Merlin did this for Ambrosius Aurelianus, the King of Britons. In his *History,* Geoffrey states that Ambrosius buried about 460 nobles who had been murdered by the Saxons at the site, and goes on to claim that Uther Pendragon (Ambrosius's brother and King Arthur's magical father) and King Constantine were also buried in the vicinity. The following is what Merlin said to King Ambrosius according to Geoffrey:

> If you [Ambrosius] are desirous to honor the burying-place of these men with an everlasting monument, send for the Giants' Dance, which is in Killaraus, a mountain in Ireland. For there is a structure of stones there, which none of this age could raise, without a profound knowledge of the mechanical

arts. They are stones of a vast magnitude and wonderful quality; and if they can be placed here, as they are there, round this spot of ground, they will stand forever.

It's interesting how much King Arthur and Merlin keep winding in and out of the mythology of Stonehenge. I do believe that these two figures existed, but not in the overblown version familiar to us from so many works of fiction.

Another legend says that the stones were bought from an Irish woman by the devil and erected on the Salisbury Plain. I find it amazing that when humankind can't explain something, more often than not we give it a negative connotation, especially if it was before the common era of Christianity. It's as if humans didn't love God before Christianity came along—not even *some* type of a creator, whatever that may be, who was greater than they were.

Now we get to the Druids. By the time they arrived on the scene, there were also smaller arrangements of stones within the large outer circle. These formations were made of a different kind of rock, called bluestone, which scientists believe came from southwestern Wales. In the 17th century, the Druids, who had been practicing in Britain for more than a thousand years prior to this, were defamed as devil worshipers given to human sacrifice and the like. (It bears repeating that whenever human beings don't understand something, evil is always attributed to it.)

When I stood there in the growing twilight, seeing these visions open up almost like a large kaleidoscope of time, I saw some white-hooded figures making their way across the plain. There seemed to be at least a hundred of them walking single file. There were no words spoken, but a very spiritual hush fell over everything—even the people I was with said that they felt it. The atmosphere, the birds, the air . . . everything became quiet, as if we were piercing the veil of a time long passed. It was obvious we were in the presence of the Druid priests.

As the Druids approached the circle, it's almost as if I could again see how this place was once whole, with all the stones in place and what I call the "altar stone" in the middle. Some of the priests stood in the circle, while others stood as sentinels on the outside, and they all began to chant in a very melodious tone. One man stepped out—the only thing that distinguished him from the rest was that he had a golden cord around his white robe. He stood with his arms straight up and began to chant very loudly, like a Greek chorus, or in Catholic ceremonies when the priest chants and the congregation answers him. I know Latin, and the chant had that flowing timbre to it but was much more primitive.

I saw the man with the golden cord take a beautiful sword out of his robe, which he then laid on the altar stone; as I watched it, it began to gleam with a golden light. Then another priest appeared and put a figurine of a nude woman with large hips and breasts on the altar next to the sword. Everyone seemed to pay homage to this idol—it's interesting to note that there was a Mother Goddess present here.

Next they joined hands and began to sing again, sounding much like a Gregorian chant. The head male turned, and everyone was seated. Another two priests came up with pouches and opened them on the altar. At first I couldn't make out what was in them, but then I saw that it was bones. It was as if they were honoring their dead.

As they sat and sang, the high priest took the sword, gestured to one of the stone doorways, and then proceeded to point at the sky. Next he went through the doorway and came back in through

the one next to it, still pointing to the sky with the sword. (I could see through some of the entrances, and I quickly realized that each one not only pointed to where the sun rose, but they pointed to different galaxies as well, including Andromeda.)

The priests sat for a long time, and then, as if on cue, each followed the leader through the doors, while looking up at the heavens. There was no human sacrifice, no bloodshed—just a group of spiritual, monklike figures in white robes giving thanks to their deity or deities and reenacting their purpose here on this earth.

All this happened in a flash, and before I could quietly utter what I was feeling, my spirit guide Francine said, "They're showing their belief that we're reincarnated time and time again, and that we come from other galaxies—the stones are symbols of our entry into this reality." *Much like the earlier Celts but even more sophisticated as far as being time travelers,* I thought.

It was as if the Druids were saying, "I will die, but I will go to the heavens and possibly recuperate there and then come back here through the doorway of life to learn." It's very much like our Gnostic Christian belief, without the astronomy attached. I came away feeling that life is a circle—sometimes we'll find ourselves back at the starting point unless we go through the doorways of life for God and learn our lessons.

———— ••◄⧓►•• ————

I must pause here to explain Francine to those of you who aren't familiar with her. Francine is my primary spirit guide, and she's been with me since I was born. (I also have a secondary guide, Raheim, who came to me later on, but he won't appear in this book.) In addition to being a trance medium and clair-voyant, I'm also *clairaudient,* which means that I'm able to *hear* Francine, which I've done since I was seven years old. Now, if you've read any of my other books, then you know that she's a great researcher and has been proven right countless times. Even things that seemed preposterous have been proven to be true over the years (there are too many of them to mention here).

Francine told me that during the spring and fall equinoxes, the people of Stonehenge would bring wheat, corn, and fruit to place on the altar stone as an offering. It was so simplistic and yet so beautiful—and not at all mysterious or frightening.

As I was leaving, I told my group to look at these round, earthen mounds that encircle Stonehenge, for they're like burial chambers. A short time later, the media reported that skeletons had been found by archaeologists in and around Stonehenge. I hate to be saying this after the fact, but I know that the people who were with me, including our guide, Peter Plunkett (who lives in Ireland), remember it all. The aspect of buried remains also goes back to the legend that Geoffrey of Monmouth relates of Stonehenge being erected as a memorial. People wanted to be buried as close to this religious and holy site as possible. The more important you were, the closer you were buried; hence, noblemen and the higher lead-ers were buried closer to the sacred site than those of lesser note.

As I've said so many times, don't just take what I say (or any-one says) for granted. Research the facts, and you'll come to the right conclusions. But don't assume that everything we don't know is wrong or evil or that we already know all the answers. A closed mind lets nothing in . . . or, for that matter, nothing out.

2
Easter Island

Easter Island has always been considered one of the most mysterious places on this planet. Located in the South Pacific, about 2,000 miles from both Chile and Tahiti (the nearest population centers), the island is not the easiest place to get to. The first European to discover the island was a Dutch admiral, Jacob Roggeveen, on Easter in 1722—thus, the name of the island.

Archaeologists say there's evidence that Polynesians discovered the island around A.D. 400; and while most scientists agree with this, some say that it was actually first inhabited by people from South America. Explorer Thor Heyerdahl, author of *Kon-Tiki,* theorized that the first inhabitants were from Peru, due to the similarity of the island's statues, called *moai,* to Peruvian stonework.

The man standing next to one of the moai is 6'4"!

The island's moai range in size from a few tons and under 4 feet tall to almost 72 feet in length and approximately 150 to 165 tons. To date, scientists have counted 887 of these statues on the island, with an average height of 13 feet and an average weight of 13 tons. Only 288 out of the 887 are at their final resting place, with the remainder either in the quarry or strewn about the island in the midst of being transported.

Today, the land, people, and language of Easter Island are all referred to as *Rapa Nui* by its inhabitants. The islanders had a written language called *Rongorongo,* which can't be completely deciphered even today. Only 26 wooden tablets containing this language still exist, and their meaning is yet to be determined.

In addition, the island contains many petroglyphs (rock carvings) which depict birds and the everyday life of the early inhabitants. These were like a diary, made to show succeeding generations how they lived and what they did in their daily life. (The movie *Rapa Nui,* directed by Kevin Reynolds, was based on some of these stone petroglyphs.)

One of the big mysteries of Easter Island is why the people stopped building the moai all of a sudden. Scientists theorize that the island's population became so large that it damaged the ecosystem to the point that it couldn't support the general populace. Some speculate that the forests on the island were cleared to the point of extinction, with the wood being used for moving the giant moai, and the land being used for agriculture. They further assert that because the wood ran out, the islanders could no longer transport the huge monoliths; hence, the sudden stoppage of work dealing with the statues.

According to the evidence, the inhabitants of Easter Island then went through a decline into a bloody civil war that some believe ended in cannibalism. It was during this time that all the statues were torn down by the islanders—it's only the recent effort of archaeologists that has put the moai in their upright positions. According to an article on the BBC's Website (**www.bbc.co.uk**), slavery and disease brought to the island by Westerners, such as smallpox and syphilis, reduced the native population to only 111 by 1877. Following the annexation of the island by Chile in 1888, however, the population has risen to approximately 3,800 today.

I don't agree with the cannibalism part, but I do know that Easter Island was home to a highly advanced civilization, and that these monoliths were made to look ominous to keep strangers out.

There's some strange correlation with the Druids only in the respect that they had their own beliefs, sacrifices to their Gods, and even a type of magic.

The moai were like silent sentinels that guarded against intruders. Imagine coming upon this island and seeing these giant, grotesque figures with their large menacing heads looking out protectively over the sea. If you were uneducated and superstitious, I'm sure you wouldn't have stopped!

Even though they don't have the symmetry that Stonehenge does, the walls and stonework of the island's inhabitants were exceptional and rivaled the masonry of Peru and Egypt. (It would be easy to believe that the moai were brought here by UFOs, as are many things we'll look at in this book, but they're not.)

3
Shangri-La

Ever since it was first made famous in James Hilton's novel *Lost Horizon*, Shangri-La has stimulated many people's imaginations. It could be because humans dearly want a place like this to exist in the world—one in which there's joy and peace, no one ever grows old, and everyone lives in harmony. I feel it's like a longing for the Other Side.

Shangri-La is supposed to be located somewhere in the Himalayan mountains in the vicinity of Tibet. (Francine says that there's a lotus-shaped city in the center of the Himalayas that's inhabited by beings from outer space. Might these be the Dropa of the stone discs and crytal skulls that were found in the mountains of China?) This mysterious place is also called Shambhala by the local Tibetan inhabitants. According to an article in *The People's Almanac #3* by David Wallechinsky, it's known as the "Hidden Kingdom," where perfect and semiperfect human beings exist who are guiding the

The lotus-flower-shaped kingdom of Shangri-La is located
in the center of the Himalayas.

evolution of humankind. (I don't want to be harsh, but they aren't
doing too good a job as far as I can tell; then again, maybe we'd
be a lot worse off if they weren't there.)

Shangri-La is supposedly protected from the outside world by psychic barriers and what the Tibetans call "snow guardians." In the early
1900s, a British major was camping in the Himalayas and saw a very
tall, lightly clad man with long blond hair who, upon seeing that he
was being watched, promptly leaped down a vertical slope and disappeared. When he mentioned this sighting, the Tibetans camping with
him showed no surprise, calmly explaining that it was one of the snow-
men who guard the sacred land of Shambhala.

A more detailed account of a type of snow guardian was given
by Alexandra David-Neel, who spent 14 years in Tibet. While making one of her many trips through the Himalayas, she saw a man moving with extraordinary speed and described him as follows:

> I could clearly see his perfectly calm impassive face and
> wide-open eyes with their gaze fixed on some invisible distant

object situated somewhere high up in space. The man did not run. He seemed to lift himself from the ground, proceeding by leaps. It looked as if he had been endowed with the elasticity of a ball, and rebounded each time his feet touched the ground. His steps had the regularity of a pendulum.

It's said that the people who have searched for Shangri-La are never heard from again. I feel that they were frozen in the perilous journey, or else they just decided to stay there. There's purportedly a monastery close by that's affected by Shambhala's residual energy; and many who have gone there have experienced incredible healing effects. Shirley MacLaine visited Tibet and told me that she felt a wonderful type of energy there.

Many historians believe that Sanskrit came from Shangri-La, while Francine says that it comes from Lemuria (which I'll discuss later in the book). Shambhala or Shangri-La is also supposed to be the source of the Kalacakra, the highest form of Tibetan mysticism. The one thing that gives this theory credence for me is that Buddha (whom I greatly respect as a messenger) preached the teachings of the Kalacakra to holy men in India. Wallechinsky states:

> Afterwards, the teachings remained hidden for 1,000 years until an Indian yogi-scholar went in search of Shambhala and was initiated into the teachings by a holy man he met along the way. The Kalacakra then remained in India until it made its way to Tibet in 1026. Since then the concept of Shambhala has been widely known in Tibet, and Tibetans have been studying the Kalacakra for the least 900 years, learning its science, practicing its meditation, and using its system of astrology to guide their lives. As one Tibetan lama put it, how could Shambhala be the source of something which has affected so many areas of Tibetan life for so long and yet not exist?

Tibetan religious texts describe the physical makeup of the hidden land in detail. It is thought to look like an eight-petaled lotus blossom because it is made up of eight regions, each surrounded by a ring of mountains. In the center of the innermost ring lies Kalapa, the capital, and the king's palace, which is composed of gold, diamonds, coral, and precious gems. The capital is surrounded by mountains made of ice, which shine with a crystalline light. The technology of Shambhala is supposed to be highly advanced; the palace contains special skylights made of lenses which serve as high-powered telescopes to study extraterrestrial life, and for hundreds of years Shambhala's inhabitants have been using aircraft and cars that shuttle through a network of underground tunnels. On the way to enlightenment, Shambhalans acquire such powers as clairvoyance, the ability to move at great speeds, and the ability to materialize and disappear at will.

The People's Almanac reports that "the prophecy of Shambhala states that each of its kings will rule for 100 years and that there will be 32 in all." As each reign passes, "conditions in the outside world will deteriorate" until the last king saves the world by leading a mighty host against evil. This sounds like Armageddon to me. In fact, could the whole concept of Armageddon have been gleaned from these ancient writings and prophecies?

According to their religious texts, Tibetan monks say that everything is happening just as it's written in the prophecy of Shambhala. They won't give out any information of what is to come, for most of them feel that we couldn't handle it or it's none of our business. This much we do know about the prophecy: The disintegration of Buddhism in Tibet, the unbelievable materialism and lack of care that goes on now throughout the world, and the wars and turmoil of the 21st century seem to fit in with what little we do know about the prophecy of Shambhala.

4
The Bermuda Triangle

The area that's been the source of so much speculation over the years spans from Miami to Bermuda to San Juan, Puerto Rico, in the Atlantic Ocean (which I'm sure was part of Atlantis, but we'll get to that in the next chapter). It's strange to realize that this area forms a pyramid-type shape, which seems to sit on a grid point linked to other points on Earth that create weird and unexplained phenomena.

Francine says that from Mexico to Egypt and from Peru to the China Sea, there are vortex points on each side of the equator that interconnect to form a grid of highly electromagnetic areas (there are approximately 12 in all) that cause strange phenomena to occur—not only in these 12 areas, but also on the interconnecting lines that tie them together. She states that the lines made travel easier for early alien visitors and were also a sort of radio or transmission grid to get information from one place to another quickly on the planet's surface, almost like the satellite system we use today.

I first heard about the Triangle when I was about 12 years old, and I'll never forget it. I was watching singer, radio personality, and TV star Kate Smith on our ten-inch Emerson TV (this would have been around 1950). A pilot was talking to her about flying over this strange place off the Florida coast. He went on to say that a silent, cylindrical object had come up alongside him while he was flying (which must have seemed really strange, since we only had prop planes back then). He said that he'd tried to contact the other object via his rudimentary radio transmission, but all he got was a "metallic-sounding" voice saying, "Get out of this area."

I thought it sounded like a fantastic story, and I gave no credence to it until years later, when a doctor friend, whom I absolutely trust, was dying of stomach cancer. He decided to take a trip to the Triangle because he'd heard that it had healing powers—and at this point in his life, he figured, what could it hurt? No matter how many times he told the story, it was always with great enthusiasm and awe.

It seems that he and three other people (one of whom was another friend of mine who held an important position at IBM) went to the approximate center of the Bermuda Triangle to go deep-sea diving. My doctor friend reported seeing a pyramid with a crystal on top under the water. He tried to get closer to it, but was repelled by what seemed to be an electrical force that went through his body.

This, I believe, wasn't just because of the pyramid (or pyra-mids—reports indicate that there may be more than one); the crys-tals also send out an electromagnetic force. I'm sure that in the next ten years or so, we'll find the remains of a pyramid with a crystal sphere as my friend saw, probably near Bimini, which is off the coast of Florida. Divers have found what looks like steps near Bimini, but for some reason, there has been no further investigation.

To make a long story short, my friend's cancer disappeared—much to the surprise of three doctors. Even though some scoffed, my friend's health was proof enough for him. I was just as excited, not only about his cure, but because without him knowing it, he'd validated what Francine had told a group of us in 1977.

She said that the Bermuda Triangle was and is an intergalac-tic highway in which people could transport themselves from one planet to another—a kind of "Beam me up, Scotty" experience from *Star Trek,* or a "stargate" like the one in the movie or TV series. People would place themselves in these tubular chutes to be sent up or down to another planet. She said the only prob-lem is that we don't have the technology to understand its con-cepts, nor do we know how to get in touch with the planet we're trying to reach so that they can employ the mechanism to uti-lize it. Imagine getting on an elevator without knowing how to push the buttons—you'd just be stuck standing there, not know-ing what to do or how to get anywhere.

There doesn't seem to be any particular time that these events happen, or any atmospheric conditions that cause them: Francine says that they're like envelopes of time that open and close. (There's one story that's been well documented in which a farmer walked out his door in Nebraska and just disappeared right in front of his entire family. For three days they could hear him calling for help in the empty air, but no one could reach him. It makes you wonder . . . sometimes these mysterious disappearances could just be cases of victims walking into these portals.) I don't want people to get the idea that this happens that often, but some claim that more than 1,000 people have been lost in the Bermuda Triangle.

No matter how many theories abound about this topic, some scientists and the U.S. Coast Guard try to sweep them under the rug as "natural phenomena." It still remains, however, that the Bermuda Triangle is one of only two places on this planet where so many lives have been lost and where such strange occurrences have come about (I'll tell you about the other one at the end of this chapter).

The famous story that brought the Triangle into the headlines involved a torpedo bomber (Flight 19) in 1945. It left Fort Lauderdale, Florida, at around two o'clock in the afternoon for a practice mission. Lt. Charles Taylor, the commander of the mission, was a very experienced pilot, and he and his crew were to fly 56 miles to Hens and Chicken Shoals to conduct practice bombing runs. When that was completed, they were to fly an additional 67 miles east, then turn north for 73 miles and finally back to their base, which was another 120 miles or so—a path that would take them on a triangular path over the sea.

After an hour and a half, a Lt. Cox picked up a radio transmission from Taylor stating that the plane's compasses weren't working. He thought he was over the Florida Keys, but Cox urged him to fly north toward Miami. Lt. Taylor became more confused and even began to think that he'd started out at the wrong point according to his compass. (The magnetic field of the underwater pyramid and crystal would naturally make all the instruments go off.)

By 4:45 P.M., it was obvious to Lt. Taylor that he was lost. At 6:20, the Navy sent out search planes (one of which was also never heard from again and was presumed to have exploded over the ocean) to find Flight 19. The last transmission from Flight 19 was heard at 7:04 P.M.

Even in calm weather, this area seems to show a high degree of electromagnetic energy on instruments. Seismographic surveys carried out across the Atlantic Ocean show that there are many deviations and unexplained contours in this part of the sea. Areas that are fairly shallow will suddenly drop off into some of the deepest chasms under any ocean. And one of the best Websites for information about the Bermuda Triangle, **www.bermuda-triangle.org**, which was founded and written by Gian J. Quasar (who's spent the last 12 years or so researching every disappearance in the Triangle and has documented them all—at least to the point that they can be documented), states that many of the "accidents" can't be explained, even when many had sent SOS signals. What's even more mysterious are those in which no SOS was sent at all.

Two of the more fascinating incidents involve the disappearance of a Super Constellation aircraft in 1954 with 42 people aboard, where no sign of wreckage or cargo was found; and the disappearance of the 590-foot freighter *Sylvia L. Ossa,* which simply vanished in 1976. In both instances, the weather was fine, yet they simply vanished without a peep from their radios, which could have sent out an SOS or at the very least advised someone that they were in trouble. The cargo in the Super Constellation had pillows, paper cups, and even life rafts, all of which were buoyant, but searches turned up no evidence of anything.

I feel that something underwater in this area becomes activated at a certain time or under certain conditions (maybe as a long-lost means of communication), and when boats or planes encounter the activated area, they become confused and get caught in the envelope of time. I asked Francine, "For God's sake, what happens to these people? Are they just trapped in some time warp?" She replied, "Of course not. We come and get them."

········<∞>········

As an aside, the Website **www.bermuda-triangle.org** states that after much skepticism in recent years, science has been probing into what causes psychic ability in people. (Good luck: I've been studied, and they still don't know how I do what I do—neither do I.) The CIA now admits, as do members of the former Soviet Union, that "psychic spying" has been engaged on both sides. You'll read it here first: I was contacted by the CIA, as my staff will testify to, and I absolutely refused to take any part in it. My role is to help people, not to be a spy. I already know what I know . . . I just sit back and wait till they find it.

Also, many people don't know that the Bermuda Triangle isn't the only place where there have been a lot of missing ships, planes, and the like. There's also an area in the China Sea known as "the Devil's Sea," which has experienced much of the same phenomena as the Bermuda Triangle—it's also interesting to note that the Bermuda Triangle has been called "the Devil's Triangle."

The Website **www.crystalinks.com** states that phenomena noted in the area of the Bermuda Triangle include a glowing green fog and glowing white water, which can be seen in satellite images. It goes on to say that even Christopher Columbus wrote about this sea in his diary. In fact, the Triangle so fooled Columbus's crew that

it almost led to mutiny (which isn't unusual, as so many have reg-
istered that all instruments go haywire in this area). This may seem
far-fetched, but who's to say that this isn't one of the reasons that
Columbus was so confused that he landed in the West Indies
instead of where he was intending to go?

The Bermuda Triangle still remains an enigma to this day—
even though researchers, marine biologists, the Coast Guard, and
the U.S. government have tried to find out what's behind the phenomena that occur there. (And this doesn't take into account the
countless private parties consisting of doctors, psychics, and scientists who have tried to figure things out.)

Odd discoveries continue to turn up around the world that
relate to the Triangle: For example, an old book by the English
explorer Percy Fawcett tells of isolated South American Indians who
described great crystals atop ruined and buried temples in the jungles of Brazil. They spoke of glowing columns and shafts of glass
and crystal, just like Edgar Cayce, the great "sleeping prophet," and
Francine have. But this information was recorded and not published
until 1950 by Fawcett's son. Colonel Fawcett left on his eighth
expedition to Brazil in 1925, and he and his party never returned,
nor was there a trace of the expedition found. (This information
came out after both Cayce and Francine presented theirs.)

I'm always confused as to why we send rockets to space when
there are so many unexplained mysteries to explore right here on
Earth. Have hope, though—with the planet tilting, most of us
will be alive to see the continents rise, or at least part of them,
so many of our questions may be answered sooner than we know.

Illustration of Atlantis, depicting the Atlanteans' abuse of natural resources.

5
The Lost Continent of Atlantis

When I was about eight years old, my grandmother first told me about a "lost continent" in the Atlantic Ocean. I haven't written much about my grandma up until this book, but let me just come out and say that she was really one of the great loves of my life. She came from German nobility and was proud of her heritage, but in a humble, not snobby, way.

Grandma Ada was 5'8" and voluptuous, a very fair blonde with big blue eyes. She'd only been educated for eight years in a convent school, yet she'd read every book in her father's enormous library and could quote entire passages from all the classics. (I somewhat inherited her memory.) Like me, Grandma Ada wasn't psychic about herself, yet she certainly healed, talked to spirits, saw visions, and so on. But my grandmother was also like Edgar Cayce as far as her "voices" were concerned. She never called them by name; she'd just say, "They told me . . ."

The reason I'm mentioning her here is because Atlantis was the subject she loved to talk about most, apart from the Other Side. She believed that she'd lived in Atlantis before; and similar to the way I feel about my beloved Kenya, she was practically addicted to the lost continent. At least I've been able to go to Kenya many times—unfortunately, my grandma was never able to go to Atlantis and experience that feeling of home. So anything she heard, read, or could elicit from her guides made her ecstatic.

When I got older and would tell Grandma Ada the things Francine had told me about Atlantis, she'd say, "Oh, that's right . . . please go on, it validates what I've heard." We'd also fill in the blanks about what the other didn't know. So what follows is the information I've gathered from my research, my hypnosis clients, my grandmother, and Francine.

Discoveries of the Lost Continent

When I visited the Greek island of Santorini not long ago, I was proudly shown book after book stating that the island is part of Atlantis. Now you might wonder how a Mediterranean island figures into a phenomenon from the *Atlantic* Ocean. Well, the eastern part of Atlantis was off the coast of Spain and Africa, and Francine says that the western part extended into the Caribbean and the Yucatán Peninsula, also encompassing the Bermuda Triangle and the Sargasso Sea. Atlantis also had small adjacent islands—of which Santorini was one—much like Catalina lies off the coast of California (yet Santorini was farther from Atlantis than Catalina is from the California coast).

The Website **www.world-mysteries.com** says that *Timaeus* and *Critias,* two of Plato's dialogues, are the only existing written records that specifically refer to Atlantis. The dialogues are conversations between Socrates, Hermocrates, Timaeus, and Critias, in which Timaeus and Critias tell Socrates of this society they knew of. This could, of course, validate Santorini's claim (being Greek) that it was originally part of Atlantis.

The dialogues tell of a conflict between the ancient Athenians and Atlanteans 9,000 years before Plato's time—so it's understandable that not much that was written in those days about anything, let alone Atlantis, has survived. Some writings by Aristotle from his own time remain, but the entire texts of what these great masters wrote has certainly not endured. Francine says that much of what was written back then was destroyed in the burning of the library at Alexandria, but even that was limited, as so much depended upon oral tradition in those days. (I find it funny that we absolutely accept the Bible to be a valid history in the oral tradition, but when you talk about such things as Atlantis or Lemuria, here come the naysaying scientists. . . .)

The continent of Atlantis seems to have first appeared approximately 500,000 years ago, and reached its prime about 12,000 to 15,000 years ago as a very artistic, scholarly, and science-oriented continent—unlike Lemuria, which had a strong spiritual base rooted in its culture (I'll talk more about Lemuria in the next chapter). And whereas Lemuria got destroyed because of a natural progression of events by Mother Nature, the highly competitive Atlanteans actually destroyed themselves as a result of their knowledge of atomic energy and nuclear physics.

In the end, when much of the continent was swept away due to earlier experiments with electromagnetic energy, most of its citizens were killed—except for a few who escaped to parts of Spain, Egypt, and the Yucatán. (Just as the Atlanteans seemingly lacked any concern about polluting the globe with their industry, if we modern humans don't stop what we're doing to our planet, we could find ourselves in the same situation. Absolute power *does* corrupt absolutely.)

Before we go any further, let's examine evidence for the existence of Atlantis as reported by **www.world-mysteries.com.**

- **A pyramid explored by Dr. Ray Brown on the sea floor off the Bahamas in 1970.** Brown was accompanied by 4 divers who also found roads, domes, rectangular buildings, unidentified metallic instruments, and a statue holding a "mysterious" crystal containing miniature pyramids. The metal devices and crystals were taken to Florida for analysis at a university there. What was discovered was that the crystal amplified energy that passed through it.

- **Ruins of roads and buildings found off Binini** *[sic]* **Island in the 1960s by the photographed and published expeditions of Dr. Mansan Valentine.** Similar underwater ruins were also photographed off Cay Sal in the Bahamas. Similar underwater ruins were found off Morocco and photographed 50 to 60 feet underwater.

- **A huge 11-room pyramid found 10,000 feet underwater in the mid Atlantic Ocean with a huge crystal top, as reported by Tony Benlk.**

- A 1977 report of a huge pyramid found off Cay
  Sal in the Bahamas, photographed by Ari Mar-
  shall's expedition, about 150 feet underwater.
  The pyramid was about 650 feet high. Mysteriously,
  the surrounding water was lit by sparkling white water
  flowing out of the openings in the pyramid and surrounded by green water, instead of the black water
  everywhere else at that depth.

- A sunken city about 400 miles off Portugal found
  by Soviet expeditions led by Boris Asturua, with
  buildings made of extremely strong concrete and
  plastics. He said, "The remains of streets suggests [sic]
  the use of monorails for transportation." He also
  brought up a statue.

- Heinrich Schliemann, the man who found and
  excavated the famous ruins of Troy (which historians thought was only a legend), reportedly left a
  written account of his discovery of a bronze vase with
  a metal unknown to scientists who examined it, in the
  famous Priam Treasure. Inside it are glyphs in Phoeni-
  cian stating that it was from King Chronos of Atlantis.
  Identical pottery was found in Tiajuanaco, Bolivia.

There are supposedly many more discoveries, but you get the
idea. There's evidently much research that reveals ancient civilizations we know nothing about. Francine said many years ago
that Atlantis had three great cataclysms in its history: the first
about 50,000 years ago; the second about 25,000 years ago; and
the third, which destroyed their civilization, about 12,000 years
ago. She went on to say that these upheavals were viewed by some

Atlanteans as warnings that they were delving into things that would demolish their civilization. Unfortunately, these "doomsday prophets" were in the minority, so they weren't listened to.

Here, it's interesting to note what **www.world-mysteries.com** has to say about Atlantis:

> The story of how these various continents became inhabited with highly advanced civilizations is a fascinating one, but after many thousands of years it all came to an end for the last time around 11,500 years ago with dramatic planetary events which sank and shifted continents and covered much of the earth with water. Clues to the history on earth before our own recently recorded history can be found in Sumerian texts.

This is pretty much the time line revealed to Grandma Ada and me by our guides, give or take 500 years. Many think that what happened to Atlantis was much like what I've often said on TV: A polar tilt puts a strain on some land masses and, along with a planetary shift, causes a crack in the continents. Lemuria and Atlantis both went under due to a polar tilt, and the result was that much of the earth was covered with water.

Atlanteans were experimenting with electromagnetic energy and gravity, which Francine says was a major cause of so much devastation. Normally a polar tilt will only precipitate volcanic eruptions, earthquakes, and some land masses to move or crack slightly, but this one was the largest in Earth's history. (And without stretching it, this could explain why we have the story of Noah and his ark.) Most of this "covering of the earth with water" can also be found in ancient Sumerian texts.

Life on Atlantis

There are many theories about what Atlanteans were like. We do know that their hierarchy basically consisted of two classes: wealthy citizens and slaves. Of course they had their rulers and various councils of elders and advisors, but these were included in the class of "citizens," most of whom were fairly wealthy, probably in large part due to the fact that there was also a slave class. Interestingly enough, slaves were treated well and respected for their talents—in fact, by today's standards, they'd be called "middle class"—and some even attained wealth in large degrees. Atlantis was a very indulgent civilization, and almost everyone shared in its bounty.

People on the lost continent had life spans of 800 years (sounds like Methuselah in the Bible) and were 8 to 12 feet tall (the Bible also speaks of giants, in Chapter 6 of Genesis). We might think that these "giants" were only fantasy, but archaeologists were shocked when more than a dozen skeletons measuring 8 to 12 feet tall were found in various locations throughout the world. The diaries of Spanish conquistadors also describe blond-haired giants 8 to 12 feet tall running around in the Andes during the conquest of the Incas. (These stories are comparable to the ones we explored earlier about the snow guardians of Shambhala.)

Atlanteans' love of the arts and culture was paramount in their lives, but so was technology—the pursuit of which led to their downfall when it got out of control. The lost continent's civilians started out pursuing creative endeavors such as philosophy, writing, sculpting, and painting, but they gradually became more technocratic and very commercialized. (On this planet right now, I see a similar situation in that we have both the spiritual faction, which goes along with aesthetics, *and* highly commercial money-making technocrats.)

Grandma Ada and I both channeled that Atlantis was a highly evolved civilization that was more sophisticated in technology than anything people today could ever dream of. For example, Atlanteans employed computers that not only held data, but also made concrete judgments based on inductive and deductive reasoning. In addition, a great deal of their technology was devoted to different forms of energy (including solar power) and what they could do with it. They harnessed gravitation, dabbled and experimented in electromagnetic forces, and utilized crystals, large and small, to focus these energies. Unfortunately, much of their knowledge has been lost to us forever.

In 1938, Edgar Cayce suggested in two readings that the Atlanteans possessed atomic power and radioactive forces. One has to ask oneself how a man who never traveled that much (and had no scientific training) could come up with words such as *radiation* and *atomic power* more than six decades ago . . . or how Francine came up with the same information before I'd ever researched Cayce.

Many theorists (including Grandma Ada and myself) believe that Atlantis was a colony of extraterrestrials—some believe they came from the Lyrian star system, while Francine says that it was Andromeda. This possibly explains why Atlanteans could levitate. And perhaps because they were from another planet, that's how they knew how to use Earth's gravitational fields. They had sky cars, nuclear-powered vehicles, and machines that cooled or warmed entire cities. They knew so much about the atmosphere that they were able to control it with powerful ionized machines, and they were the ones who constructed the portal in the Bermuda Triangle.

They also had some control over weather, earthquakes, and volcanic eruptions, although at the time of their existence, our planet was even more violent in nature than it is today. This control over weather contributed greatly to the Atlantean economy by helping to produce bumper crops that would put our puny vegetables to shame. In addition, their preservation of food was stunning: While under hypnotic regression, one of my clients said that they "saw" that the Atlanteans used a type of alum that would preserve food for years and never destroy its taste.

Atlanteans had breathtaking gardens and waterways, almost like a canal system, which went through and around many of their cities. Their homes and public buildings were spectacular in their beauty: Many lived in pyramid-type structures; in fact, the Atlanteans made pyramids the focal point of their civilization. My grandmother and I both intuited that some of their pyramids were holistic centers, as well as communication hubs that were used as relay or phone stations from which people could send and receive messages instantly. These structures could be built speedily, using a type of antigravitational rod, and the technology was carried over to ancient Egypt and other cultures and then lost. Most Atlantean architecture contained many columns and arches, designs that were also embraced by the Greeks and Romans.

People on the lost continent didn't bury their dead; instead they cremated them, using a type of laser energy focused through crystals. They built large pyramids for healing, again using crystals. Their healing centers had what we might call a massage table today, on which the ill person would lie down, and multiple crystals would be focused on him or her to employ light and color therapy, laser surgery, and magnetic energy. Healing technicians (doctors) would come in with different types of ointments and balms or drugs, depending upon the treatment needed, and use the crystals in the healing process.

Atlanteans also had a type of machine for the rejuvenation of the body that employed electromagnetic energy through crystals, which helped in life extension . . . and, as I stated, life spans in Atlantis were usually very long. In addition, they used this machine for the diagnosis of maladies, because the person would go into a type of chamber and the machine would "read" the person's aura, almost doing a magnetic x-ray (but more sophisticated than an MRI) that provided comprehensive pictures of the body.

Artificial organs were used for transplants when needed, but toward the end, when their civilization became more corrupt, Atlanteans began to experiment with animals and humans in bizarre and dangerous ways, even to the point of trying to make man-beast combinations. Francine says that many of our mythological creatures, such as the Satyr or the Minotaur, derived from stories of these experiments. It started with just trying to make different creatures out of two distinct species, but deteriorated from there.

As time progressed, it seems that the Atlanteans used their technology to attain more power, and not just for healing and staying young. As in all things great and small, greed became its own master—so they began to use crystals to enhance their technology and barter more for bigger and better things. It seems that the power of the crystal was then used for destructive purposes such as wiping out groups of people who didn't please the ruling classes. (Maybe these are the flying machines described in Sanskrit texts, with death rays that wreaked havoc and destroyed thousands of people.)

Whatever their outcome, Atlanteans still had the use of nuclear and magnetic energy and enjoyed tremendous healing capabilities, and their scientific knowledge hasn't been equaled

6
Lemuria

Lemuria, a continent that existed in the Pacific Ocean around the same time as Atlantis, seems to have become forgotten, even though it was Atlantis's spiritual opposite. Lemurians believed that materialism was not an end in itself; instead, they placed more emphasis on healing, art, music, and spirituality.

The citizens of Lemuria, or Mu, as it's known in some circles, were involved with clairvoyance and telepathy, which was accepted as the norm rather than the exception. Mu was probably as close to a Shangri-La as any continent we could ever know in this world. Many believe (and Francine concurs) that *this* is where Sanskrit came from. (The Essenes and the entire Gnostic movement also date back to this time.)

While Atlanteans were said to be very tall, fair, and Nordic looking, Lemurians were shorter and darker. Both seemed to have unsurpassed beauty, and according to Francine, they had close-to-perfect DNA. However, Lemuria wasn't as highly populated as Atlantis, and the people dressed very much alike—almost Christlike, in brown or gray robes and sandals. They lived very simply, and the well-being of family and friends and the betterment of the whole was the goal. Like the Druids, Lemurians were interested in the movement of the stars and the equinoxes. Francine says that they were superb at planting, and grew fruits and vegetables the size of most people's heads.

Lemurian homes were shaped like pyramids, just like Atlantean domiciles. (You'll notice that pyramids show up a lot in this book—after all, look at the tepee of the American Indian: Isn't it pyramid shaped? This shape seems to be efficient, as it can keep the warmth in and the cold out.)

However, the people of Mu weren't as keen on technology as Atlanteans; instead, they were more into herbs, naturalistic and holistic cures, and the laying on of hands. The closest thing they had to a leader would have been someone like the Dalai Lama, or a shamanistic person who had elevated him- or herself to spiritual ascension. Like the American Indian or the Masai culture in Africa, there was always a wise man or woman to whom people could go to for advice.

I never cease to be amazed that purity of the soul originates from a single mind in a group, yet it often leads to someone rising up to become the false savior. Amazingly, this didn't happen in Lemuria. Knowing what the world is like today, this is probably the first and last time that this could exist.

In my church, the Society of Novus Spiritus, we let everyone find their own God-center, and hopefully we walk together, seeking our truth, listening to Christ's words of "Seek and ye shall find." Truth, not dogma, will bind people together in a common search to glorify God. So perhaps this was the way Mu was, as Francine says.

Lemurians had their religious ceremonies, yet they also enjoyed high festival days that celebrated every equinox, when they would dance and sing and even drink a mild ale made out of a cornmeal substance. Marriage was with one person; families were the primary units; and farming, weaving, building, and cooking were the main occupations. Although there was a lot of community living, with everyone pitching in to till the fields and care for each other's children, it wasn't anything like a commune. Instead, families lived near each other for necessity and survival. And because there was so much peace and harmony, there wasn't much crime on Mu.

Many now-extinct animals also lived on this continent. A feline, which was bigger than our domestic cat and with sharper features, was a favorite pet, as was a type of dog that looked like a jackal and was much greater in size yet very docile. Elephants (somewhat smaller than today's variety) were used in work; and there was also a type of large bovine creature that produced milk.

Now, I don't believe in communism because it destroys initiative, but it *can* be successful if everyone shares an equal interest in furthering their own spirituality. If there's no fanatical dictator who takes all the money, it can work. Lemuria had a form of communism in which all were equal, but Mu didn't get corrupt or become undisciplined—maybe because it cracked and went under quickly in a polar tilt! I'd like to believe that it would have stayed pure, and not being cynical, I often wonder if outsiders had been allowed to come in (which they weren't), whether it might have changed the Lemurians' views or made them more materialistic. They evidently felt that, too, since very few people were allowed to settle on the continent and could only stay if they got with the program, so to speak.

The Urantia Book, published by the Urantia Foundation, presents more information about Lemuria, but like many written materials on the subject, it seems to be rather vague. Francine says that most writings about Mu are in Sanskrit texts, and many are quite specific. Lemuria's culture lasted about 10,000 or 12,000 years, during which time the outside world didn't touch it too often. Their writings, spirituality, art, and music progressed, but their materialism didn't.

Lemurians kept to themselves, which probably contributed to the continuation of their static commercial culture, their total dependence upon themselves, and the lack of perversion and influence from the outside world. They had the occasional visit from Atlanteans, but by and large, Atlantis left them alone.

I'm sure that Lemurians also had reciprocation from outer-space beings because, just like with Atlantis, certain Sanskrit texts tell of flying machines. If such creatures did visit, then this would explain the aircraft and other inventions that have slipped into modern consciousness courtesy of a select few who were privileged to view some of these texts. The problem is that the people who go on to interpret these texts seem to become so mesmerized by the information that they don't want to leave it behind.

Another reason for the limited information on Lemuria is because Sanskrit is a very difficult language to learn and translate, and many say that the monks of Tibet aren't letting all the texts they guard out for public viewing. That makes sense, especially when the information may be highly controversial, and they have the Chinese government looking over their shoulder. Trust me, when the time is right, the information will be forthcoming, but not with the world in as much turmoil as it is today.

Francine says that every 12,000 to 15,000 years, the polar tilt causes continents to rise and fall, so Lemuria and Atlantis will rise again around the years 2020 to 2030.

Part II

Strange Creatures

An example of the form a tulpa might take.

7
Tulpas

You may be wondering why I've put several legendary creatures together in one chapter, but as we go along, I'll show you how they fall under the same heading of thoughts becoming things, or what we call *tulpas*.

When writer and explorer Alexandra David-Neel journeyed through Tibet, one of the many well-known but mystical techniques she studied was that of tulpa creation. In *Body, Mind & Spirit: A Dictionary of New Age Ideas, People, Places, and Terms,* authors Eileen Campbell and J. H. Brennan write:

> A *tulpa,* according to traditional Tibetan doctrines, is an entity created by an act of imagination, rather like the fictional characters of a novelist,

except that tulpas are not written down. [Alexandra] David-Neel became so interested in the concept that she decided to try to create one.

The method involved was essentially intense concentration and visualization. David-Neel's tulpa began its existence as a plump, benign little monk, similar to Friar Tuck. It was at first entirely subjective, but gradually, with practice, she was able to visualize the tulpa out there, like an imaginary ghost flitting about the real world.

In time the vision grew in clarity and substance until it was indistinguishable from physical reality—a sort of self-induced hallucination. But the day came when the hallucination slipped from her conscious control. She discovered that the monk would appear from time to time when she had not willed it. Furthermore, her friendly little figure was slimming down and taking on a distinctly sinister aspect.

Eventually her companions, who were unaware of the mental disciplines she was practicing, began to ask about the "stranger" who had turned up in their camp—a clear indication that a creature which was no more than solidified imagination had definite objective reality.

At this point, David-Neel decided things had gone too far and applied different lamaist techniques to reabsorb the creature into her own mind. The tulpa proved very unwilling to face destruction in this way so that the process took several weeks and left its creator exhausted.

After I read this account, I was so fascinated that I began to explore this further. *How could this be?* I wondered. I already knew that thoughts are things, but this gave new meaning—and even a frightening aspect—to affirmations.

Through my research, I ran across a group of six people in England who were also able to create a tulpa some years ago. Every night, Marian Hallsley gathered her friends together in order to try to contact the dead. These people weren't uneducated or frivolous—among them were a journalist, a scientist, a dentist, a doctor, and a businessman. After numerous attempts to connect with the deceased, they still had no success. Mediums were even called in, yet no one could manage to contact anyone on the Other Side.

One night Marian had an idea: The group would make up their own spirit! So night after night, this gathering took painstaking details to bring an entity into being. They gave him a birth date, a birthplace (Liverpool), and a name (Edward Howard). His height was noted; as was his exact weight, hair color, and mustache. They gave him a wife and two children, and an occupation as a banker; they even determined that he wore a bowler hat and a tweed suit, smoked a pipe, and carried a walking stick. The group began to create a childhood for Edward and imagine his thoughts. As one of the six participants remarked, "We know more about Edward than we do about each other."

One night, after almost a year and a half of constructing the full scope of Edward's life, the table at which the gathering sat began to move so violently that they all jumped away from it. Sure enough, there was Edward Howard in all his glory! The group, with their unbelievable concentration, had created a tulpa. This story has been well documented—I even talked to Minnie Bridges, who was a student at the Spiritualist college that Sir Arthur Conan Doyle frequented, and she corroborated that she had also seen Edward; in fact, many of the area mediums were called upon to get rid of him.

Now, I don't mean to give you any fear of creating a tulpa, and I should mention that this process only seems to work for those who have too much time on their hands; in addition, the atmosphere and conditions have to be just right. Tibet would be an ideal place because of its mysticism and meditative practices, as would England, for its fog helps conduct electrical energy (in this case, mental energy). So again, the idea that thoughts are things takes on a new meaning!

The Loch Ness Monster

The first tulpa we'll explore is the Loch Ness monster, or "Nessie," as she's called in Ireland and Scotland. When I went to the British Isles, I heard an old tale that relates the story of St. Columba, who started the first monastery in Scotland. In the mid-sixth century, St. Columba supposedly spotted the monster, and from this account, the word began to spread and articles were written—and the famous picture that looks like a prehistoric dinosaur with its neck jutting out of the water sprang up (it has since been proven to be a hoax).

It's strange that Nessie wasn't really news until the 1930s, yet legend says that she's always been residing in the loch. Rupert T. Gould was instrumental in introducing the monster to the world with *The Case for the Sea Serpent,* in which he noted 51 accounts of sightings of Nessie; Constance Whyte's work *More than a Legend* also helped revive interest in the monster in the 1950s.

In fact, an entire book could be devoted just to the Nessie photos, films, and video—yet so far, all the "evidence" has turned out to be a hoax or inconclusive. Scientists and experts have yet to come up with any proof that the monster exists, even though Loch Ness itself has been sounded, sonared, radared, and dragged for years, and cameras have been set up there day and night.

The best and probably most famous and thorough search of all was "Operation Deepscan" in 1987. Here, scientists swept the loch with 24 boats, each of which was fitted with a scanning sonar device, and they worked in unison to cover the entire under-water area of Loch Ness. While they did encounter some "contacts," nothing concrete came of the investigation. In July 2003, the BBC reported that a team of researchers proved once and for all that there is no monster in the lake. Using 600 separate sonar beams and satellite navigation equipment, they scanned the entire body of water and didn't find anything.

Even though nothing of a provable nature has been found, the sightings still continue. It's interesting that when a war or any other major world event is going on, there seems to be no sign of Nessie—

but let it be a slow news week, and suddenly, there she is! The famous photograph I mentioned earlier was supposedly taken during one of these times of interest, and the photographer has since confessed that it was a hoax in which he used a small model.

However, no matter how often science debunks Nessie, believers keep popping up and more sightings keep occurring. What's the explanation for this? Well, clearly there *is* a type of monster—possibly even one with a dinosaur-shaped body and head—but I believe with all my heart that Nessie is a tulpa that has been created by a belief, many books, and supposed sightings. She's real, in a manner of speaking, because thousands of thoughtforms have helped create her.

Sasquatch

Now let's go to Sasquatch—or the Abominable Snowman, Bigfoot, or yeti—all of which are names that have been given to a large, hairy, half-man/half-beast creature. It's interesting to note that in various parts of the world he's called different things, yet he always seems to fit the same description. Sasquatch has supposedly been sighted several times—there are even famous films, blurry as they may be, that have captured this apeman-like figure.

Many who have claimed to have seen Sasquatch describe him as being six to ten feet tall and weighing anywhere from 500 to 800 pounds. I don't know about you, but a difference of four feet and 300 pounds is not exactly specific—nevertheless, we can't discount that there have been many sightings, just like with Nessie. The difference is that Sasquatch appears to have crossed many continents,

TULPAS

while Nessie seems to be centered mostly around and in Loch Ness in Scotland. But like Nessie, the popularity of Bigfoot waxes and wanes. Every few years we get very excited about these sightings, and then for some reason he fades back into obscurity.

For example, in 1998, American mountaineer Craig Calonica reported that while descending from a campsite at a high altitude on Mount Everest, he spotted two strange creatures that had thick, shiny, black fur. They were walking on two legs just like humans, yet their arms were longer than human arms and they had very large heads. Craig swears that it was no animal he's ever seen, and he's pretty much seen them all—he believes he saw two yetis. Craig was accompanied by his Nepali cook who also saw the creatures.

Researchers are still doing their fieldwork, and as late as October of 2000, a group became convinced that Sasquatch truly is alive—14 of them tracked the elusive beast for a week and supposedly found an imprint of a hair-covered body lying on its side, reaching over to get some fruit. (I don't want to seem unscientific or stupid, but how did they know it was reaching for fruit, even with thermal imaging that confirmed that the body print was only hours old?)

Doubters of the existence of Sasquatch certainly abound, but there are also many skeptics who have turned into believers. Jimmy Chilcutt, who is highly regarded by agents of the FBI and state and local law enforcement for his expertise in fingerprints, set out to prove once and for all that there was no Sasquatch, yet he ran across some footprint castings that rocked his skepticism.

Chilcutt compared primate footprints and fingerprints with the castings of supposed Bigfoot imprints, and he found that there were so many significant differences that now he doesn't dismiss the existence of this creature. However, he also hasn't come to a conclusive finding. As he says, "We'll never know for sure until a specimen is collected."

Some of the eyewitness accounts that keep repeating throughout the bulk of the sightings have to do with Sasquatch's bizarre antics, which run the gauntlet from relatively benign (such as throwing small stones) to more aggressive (such as shaking vehicles, slapping or shoving dwellings, hurling large rocks, and chasing people). Loud, resonant calls and overwhelming, even eye-watering odors have also frequently been reported by observers, according to John Bindernagel in his book *North America's Great Ape: The Sasquatch*.

Debunkers and skeptics all seem to agree that Sasquatch is some form of bear. They also like to point out that the aforementioned behavior can be tracked to chimpanzees, gorillas, and orangutans, who many times act in the same way. The stories go on and on, including some downright hoaxes (why do people want to perpetuate a hoax anyway?).

There's been more written about this creature than there ever has been about Nessie, but I feel that's reasonable. Like gnomes and fairies, every culture seems to have embraced the large, hairy beast that no one has been able to prove (or, I might add, disprove) exists. From Florida with its skunk ape (called so because of its smell); to Australia, where it's called *yoser;* to the *mapinguary,* which is the Bigfoot of Brazil, all places seem to have their own legends and stories of a Sasquatch-like beast.

The Leviathan

According to the dictionary, a leviathan is a large sea creature of unknown origin that has been reportedly seen many times by early seafaring men. People assume that it was actually a whale or a large shark, but this doesn't hold much weight when you realize that ancient mariners used to spend their lives on the seas, so they'd certainly know the difference between a whale or a shark and a leviathan.

Granted, shipwrecked sailors would often become desperate enough to drink seawater, which would then dehydrate them and cause hallucinations and death. (However, this doesn't explain the hundreds of able-bodied, sane men who came back from sea with tales of a giant, mysterious monster.)

The manatee may fit into tales that are accompanied by delirium, for scientists have ascertained that that's what sailors thought were mermaids. Now I don't know about you, but to my eyes, a manatee is about as far away from a beautiful, shapely woman with a tail as a cow is from a tree. Having said that, I can also see where sailors on the ocean for years or months without female companionship could make anything look like whatever they wanted it to after being so deprived.

Ancient Viking chroniclers also tell tales of giant sea creatures. Now, I'm sure that many of these tales are true, but I'm also convinced that there were monstrous squid involved. Recently such a creature washed up on shore in Australia, just as they have on other continents. Scientists have found specimens up to 60 feet in length—and many of us can recall having seen ancient pictures of mariners fighting huge sea monsters with tentacles.

I feel that we don't see these squid because they stay only in the deepest parts of the oceans, which are the only places that can provide enough food to support their weight and girth. Unlike many large whales, which consume plankton and krill for their main diet, squid live on fish and sea animals—and I'm sure that if they were hungry enough, they'd attack anything or anyone to get food.

As you can see, the mind is a powerful thing, and it has the ability to bring thought to a type of life force on its own. This is how legends, stories, and very strong beliefs create tulpas.

Lilith, the fairy queen
of the Underworld

8
The Fairy World

Francine says that there's a subphylum of creatures that helps Mother God keep the world in balance as much as She can: fairies. Now, I'll buy a lot of things, but trust me, I've *never* bought into fairies.

I think everyone has a right to their own beliefs—and I'm also aware that almost every country except America seems to believe in elves, gnomes, little people, leprechauns, or fairies. (It does seem strange that so many cultures share tales of creatures such as this. Why would they all exist in various cultures as pretty much the same type of creatures?) So I've always said, "To each his own." It's certainly helped my skepticism over the years to never say never. I guess it's like Jesus said: "Blessed are those who have not seen yet have believed."

Then in 1977, I went to Ireland. I was riding in a horse-drawn jaunting car in a beautiful park near one of the lakes of Killarney when I happened to catch something out of the corner of my eye. Lo and behold, it was a fairy—with wings and all!—on an oleander bush. She was beautifully formed, had golden hair, and wore a wonderful blue gossamer dress. I blinked and looked again; she didn't pay me any mind, but instead went gently from leaf to leaf and flower to flower. I screamed at the driver, "I just saw a fairy!"

He looked back at me as if I were the stupid one. "Of course," he replied, "they're all over the place."

My second husband, who was with me at the time, was of Irish descent and used to tease me about my lack of belief in little people, fairies, and the like; I'd always tell him that he was nuts. I looked over and saw this "I told you so" grin on his face . . . and promptly whacked him one.

I'm sure that everyone remembers reading about what happened years ago when they tried to build an airport runway across fairy circles at the Shannon Airport in Ireland. Everything went so badly for months—machinery broke down or just wouldn't work, and people got sick and injured—that they abandoned the project and went in a different direction away from the circles . . . at which point everything progressed quite smoothly. If you discuss this with the locals who live near the airport, they'll simply admit that you shouldn't mess with fairy circles.

In ancient times, fairies seem to have been more evil, but as time has gone on, they've morphed into kindly, mischievous, and caring little people. There was nothing evil about this sprite I saw;

in fact, if she'd been bigger, I would have thought she was an angel, thanks to the golden-white glow around her. Francine told me later that I'd actually seen poor, defamed Lilith herself (who I'll talk about in a bit). I know what I saw; even now I'd take a lie-detector test because I just don't go around seeing things (unless I'm asked to tune in on a ghost or happen to bump into one).

So be my guest, and take or leave what I saw. Personally, I'll always cherish this beautiful visual, which proved the old saying to be true: There are more things in heaven and earth than humans can even imagine.

A demon frightening some pious folk.

9
Demons

I'd like to take the opportunity to clear up the mystery of why we keep hearing about a certain subculture—be it in story, myth, or urban legend—called "demons."

In other books, I've talked about the seven different levels on the Other Side, each of which has its specific occupational level, as it were. Well, we also have seven levels on the earthly plane: First is the level we exist on in life; second is the fairy level; the third contains gnomes and elves; the fourth has mythological creatures such as unicorns, flying horses (like Pegasus), the white sacred bull, or the Cyclops; and the fifth, sixth, and seventh are the lower levels, which are said to contain horrible creatures.

It's not that the lower levels really exist, but so many people have concerned themselves with such creatures that they've become tulpas, like Bigfoot, Nessie, and Sasquatch. For example:

- The ancient Greeks believed in three types of vampiric demigoddesses—the Lamia, the Mormo, and the Empusa. The Lamia and Mormo supposedly drank babies' blood (the Lamia also attacked pregnant women), while the Empusa sexually seduced young men and then killed them by drinking their blood and eating their internal organs.

A demon tempting a couple.

- In India, Pacu Pati (whose name literally means "master of the herd") is believed to be the ruler of all vampiric spirits, witches, and ghosts; some Hindu traditions also consider him the god of death, like Yama in classic Hindu literature. Some of the uneducated in India still consider Pacu Pati an all-powerful force, for he supposedly can take possession of dead corpses and animate them like his own body—which smacks of "undead" vampires and zombies.

- The word *nightmare* comes from *night* and the old Anglo-Saxon word *mare,* which was considered to be a demonic spirit who attacked people in their sleep. In England, people believed that this spirit would sit on people's chests and give them tuberculosis (which was a way to explain illness in the Middle Ages).

The subject of demons has always been very controversial and has been around as long or longer than recorded history. It seems that whatever humans can't explain—be it volcanic eruptions, illnesses, plagues, famines, or acts of nature—was said to be caused by "evil spirits." Apparently, humankind's only way of explaining the misfortune that would descend upon us was an evil entity or an angry God that had to be appeased by offerings or sacrifice.

Considering the suffering we humans have gone through in our history, it's understandable that we've made up our own mythology to explain the injustices of life. Of course I believe evil exists in the world, but I don't believe that it's related to anything we'll discuss in this chapter. Yet human beings seem to almost *need* to blame the world's follies on an unseen malevolent force rather than taking responsibility for their own lives.

Here are explanations for some commonly known demons:

Lilith

Lilith, whom we hear about in the Talmud and Bible, was believed to make women miscarry or be barren, and to cause men to be impotent. (Notice here that even when it's negative, the female is the giver and taker of life.) Her father was the sky god Anu, the prime mover and creator of the universe.

In the *Alphabet of Ben Sirah,* Lilith was said to be the first wife of Adam and made of dust like him. She demanded equality with Adam, which he refused, so then she supposedly consorted with demons and gave birth to demonic children. (I don't know about you, but this sounds like another way to make women inferior to men.) Legend has it that if a person wore a protective amulet, Lilith wouldn't harm him or her.

Out of this belief and fear of death or destruction, the amulet—which is anything that's supposed to bring good luck and protection to the wearer—was born. We still use amulets to this day when we don our crucifixes, crystals, rosary beads, and so on. I don't believe that the amulet has any power by itself; instead, its potency comes from the energy we give it and what it has symbolized through history. For example, I wear a Templar cross (which is equal on all sides) because it's the oldest Gnostic cross there is, and I've given it energy.

DEMONS

Archaeologists have dug up countless amulets over the years; the British Museum in London even exhibits some that supposedly protected women against the infamous Lilith. (Francine says that Lilith wasn't evil, but actually rules over the fairies and lower phyla of the earth.)

Banshees and Sirens

Celtic lore speaks of many spirit women—good *and* evil. One of the most famous in Ireland and parts of Scotland is the *banshee* (or *beansidhe*)—and it's said that when someone is close to death, the screech of the banshee can be heard. I've been over to the British Isles and have talked to some very smart, educated people who have heard these wails, only to later discover that a loved one had died. This happened so often that I asked Francine about it. I found her explanation a little hard to swallow at first, but it makes more sense than a lot of other things.

She told me that when someone's going to die, his or her psyche or soul will know that its passing is imminent. The soul lets out a psychic scream, even before the person passes, and because of the dense air and dew in the British Isles, the "silent" scream is often heard—which has been attributed to the banshee. (I think we can also insert here the ancient sirens and mermaids of lore who have purportedly lured sailors to their death on hidden rocks or shoals with their noisy screeching or songs. Could this not be a warning from the mariners' own subconscious that rocks or a narrow passage lie ahead?)

The Incubus and Succubus

The *incubus* and *succubus* are male and female demons, respectively, that seduce persons of the opposite sex, usually at night or while sleeping. These myths actually started in the "Burning Times," in which women were routinely burned at the stake.

Believers thought that the succubus would appear to a male as a beautiful woman and seduce him; then, after the sexual act was over, she'd turn into an ugly hag. Meanwhile, the incubus disguised himself as a handsome man who typically preyed on a lonely woman—after intercourse, he'd turn into a type of "demon" or warlock (male witch). The actions of the incubus or succubus were said to make their sufferers go crazy.

Inventing the incubus and succubus conveniently explained unwanted pregnancies, children born out of wedlock, birth deformities, and so on. Belief in them also enabled inquisitors to look for any moles or birthmarks that would show that people had been seduced by these witchlike demons. It's almost as if people were caught in a mass frenzy that caused suggestibility; when pandemonium broke out, it gave the Church every reason to burn these hapless souls. It's tragic that such hysteria ran rampant during these times.

Gargoyles

Many of the gargoyles that you see outside of churches seem to be copies of demigods. Gargoyles are mythical creatures (also called "grotesques") that were carved by masons as spouts to drain water off the roofs of buildings. The word *gargoyle* comes from the French word *gargouille,* which means "throat" (we also get the words *gargle* and *gurgle* from that root).

Gargoyles were an architectural feature in ancient Roman buildings, such as those found in Pompeii, and were used to ward off evil. From the way they look, it's almost as if they put evil outside to ward it off from coming inside. Personally, I've always thought that it looked garish to have these so-called mythological figures outside a house of worship.

＊＊＊

I really don't think it's necessary to concern ourselves with myths that have been handed down from a world that didn't have the science or knowledge to explain why things really happened. In other words, why worry about a world of demons that had nothing better to do than aggravate us, and that was used to frighten the masses? Again, what we can't seem to explain, we have a tendency to put a negative spin on . . . as if we don't have enough to genuinely worry about, such as AIDS, wars, killings, abductions, or the proverbial germ that always seems to elude science.

Medicine changes, myths mutate; after all, for years people with epilepsy were looked on stupidly as being possessed. And in the early days, when they didn't know about genes or even germs, everything was blamed on the "bad humors" that entered the body. People were bled to get the bad humors out—and some, like George Washington, were bled to death in such efforts. It seems that humans back then couldn't escape being either cursed or demonically possessed. (Would you believe that even in this day and age I still have people ask me if they're cursed? They just don't want to take responsibility for the course of study they chose for this life in order to perfect for God.)

Demons certainly don't enter our bodies, but negative energy or a toxic person *can* make us feel drained and sick. I've often said at my lectures that germs don't make us sick, but people and situations can—that is, we can't "digest" life, so we get a stomachache; or we take on too much, so we get backaches, and so on. Our bodies speak to us literally: Keep saying someone broke your heart, and you'll end up with heart difficulties; if someone makes your "blood boil," you'll get high blood pressure. I don't want to make you overly self-conscious, but stop using negative phrases that your body responds to.

To show you how smart I am (keep in mind, I've never claimed to be psychic about myself), I didn't realize until much later that my last husband was strangling me with his pressure. After the divorce, my doctor found a tumor in my throat (benign, thank God) that was wound around my vocal cords. Since I don't smoke and have always had a husky voice, as have all the women in my family, I wasn't concerned about my throat, but the doctor found the growth in a routine exam. (I knew that God, Francine, and my angels had guided him to find it.) Later, I offhandedly asked him what the outcome would have been. He said, "It would have slowly strangled you."

Now, you could call dark entities like my ex-husband "demons," but they're merely souls that have separated from God out of vanity. They may drive us crazy with their uncaring and sociopathic personalities, but they're here to make us learn.

I really believe that we'll never know it all, but the beauty of life here and on the Other Side is to keep researching God and the world's mysteries. As Francine says, "If you can think of the question, the answer will become available to you." So read and explore, and you'll find enlightenment and the answers to all your questions.

A witch hunt.

10

Witches and Werewolves

Many historians theorize that stories of vampirelike beings, demons, witches, and fairies started in ancient Babylonian, Sumerian, and Assyrian mythologies—which, as I stated in *Mother God,* is where much of our Bible originated. Yet how in the name of God—literally—we get so far from the truth can sometimes elude me, until I remember that each of us brings our own experiences and perceptions to the so-called party of life.

In the next two chapters, I continue exploring the many metaphors that humankind has created in order to try to explain a world that often makes no sense at all.

Witches

Witches have been misunderstood, and many times maligned, throughout the centuries. We envision an old hag over a cauldron whipping up a brew to bring destruction to an unfortunate victim, with her "familiar" black cat, who could take orders from the devil (or the witch could take the form of a cat herself to bestow bad luck upon anyone whose path she crossed).

This is all antiquated legend and superstition—yet much of witches' bad PR comes from prior centuries in which countless people were killed in Europe thanks to the Inquisition, and from Salem, Massachusetts, the site of the various witch trials. (I don't suppose it occurred to the Church that if you get rid of all the women, you're not going to have many members.)

Now, I'm sure that there have been many evil people over time who have tried to cast black-magic spells—which is dangerous because what we send out comes back—but true Wiccans follow one of the oldest religions there is.

I can't say enough here that ignorance is *not* bliss, so before you make a judgment, go back to the original tenets of the religion witches subscribe to. While modern Wicca was formed in the 1950s, it has its roots in an ancient pantheistic religion that believes that all of nature contains God; and it's also very attached to the female principle or Goddess.

Wiccans *do* employ spells, but true practitioners use them for positive ends, such as bringing rain when there's a drought, healing cattle or livestock, or dealing in herbs and folk medicines to create wellness. People don't realize that affirmations are actually part of a type of Wiccan ritual—these white witches believe that what we repeat comes to us, and we're programmed for good.

Of course, in any group, you always have a few who stand out and make the rest look bad. (For example, "TV psychic" Miss Cleo demeaned all of us true psychics.) A Wiccan who abuses her or his power is usually a dark entity who has flagrantly misused the energy of positive programming.

Am I a witch, or do I want to be? No, but I do admire their tenacity to keep their beliefs alive. And even though I've never cast a spell or been a Wiccan, I've read and researched enough of their literature to know that the true Wiccan is geared toward goodness, harmony, and protecting the planet.

———···❮∞❯···———

Whenever I think about witches, I remember Grandma Ada telling me about a little gnomelike man she encountered as a child in the Black Forest of Germany. He'd meet her in the overgrown areas of her family's estate, where he taught her all about the medicines and herbs found in the forests.

When anyone who knew Grandma Ada was sick, they'd come to her for cures and poultices. (I always have visions of her taking me to a forest or park in Kansas City and putting plants in her apron. I greatly regret that I never had her teach me more about what she knew.) Now, was it the knowledge from her little childhood friend, her own psychic ability, or her unquenchable faith in God that was responsible for her healing gifts? Frankly, who knows and who cares—it worked.

Yet I'm sure that if my grandmother had been born in an earlier time, she would have been burned as a witch. Thankfully, she was protected—how ironic—by the Jesuits and priests. She had many letters from Bishop Sheen, which I hope to find someday. I say this without any humility: She was a modern-day saint. There was no one whom she didn't want to help, and someday I'll publish her letters to me, which are priceless. She's been my role model my whole life, and truly the wind beneath my sails.

Werewolves

The term *lycanthrope,* which is used to describe the werewolf phenomenon, originated from a Greek myth in which Zeus visited the court of King Lycaon disguised as a traveler. The ruthless king wanted to find out if the traveler was a god or a man, so he made plans to kill the stranger. Zeus was outraged, destroying the king's palace and condemning King Lycaon to spend the rest of his life as a wolf. Thus, the term *lycanthropy* (*lykos* = wolf, and *anthropos* = man), describing the transformation into a wolf, came into being.

The modern werewolf legend is said to have begun in Germany in 1591 when, after a multitude of apparent attacks, the townspeople cornered a wolf with some dogs, and the wolf suddenly took the shape of a local man. The man was subsequently accused of the murders of several townspeople, including his own son; under torture, he confessed to all the crimes and was executed. The incident grew into legend, and stories soon spread all over Europe about the presence of werewolves. (You must remember that we're talking a time when people were largely ignorant, and the Catholic Church was doing its own purge with the deadly Inquisition. The general populace was very superstitious, and "witch hunting" was starting to come into vogue—consequently, innocent people were tortured and confessed to crimes that they didn't commit.)

It wasn't until 1621, when clergyman and scholar Robert Burton published *Anatomy of Melancholy,* that people began to look at werewolves differently. Mr. Burton believed that lycanthropy was a form of madness, and he blamed everything from demons to witches to poor diet and even bad air. This caused the scientific community to look at the werewolf phenomenon as a mental illness rather than a physical transformation.

When I began to write this chapter, my mind was stimulated by what Francine had told a group of us more than 30 years ago. (Thank God I was able to find it in the archives!) She said that most of the time, people who thought they were werewolves were in a state induced by a type of hallucinogen found in wheat, laudanum, and belladonna (nightshade), which were remedies to treat a number of ailments years ago. The combination of these drugs then gave rise to the popular myth of the werewolf who would change with the full moon and have to go out and kill for blood.

In the course of my research for this book, I found out that these substances, along with ergot-tainted bread (ergot is a type of fungus), can cause the same hallucinogenic effects as LSD. (In fact, in France in 1951, people who had eaten this polluted bread had horrible visions of being attacked and turning into beasts.) I accept this explanation totally, rather than believing that God made one of His creations turn into something horrible like a werewolf. Medical doctors have also told me that in some people, a werewolf-type effect can be created if they can't get enough water—in their delirium, such individuals have been known to go after any liquid . . . even human blood.

I also discovered that there's a rare genetic disorder called *porphyria* that results in a deficiency of heme, or the iron-containing portion of hemoglobin, and it stimulates the growth of body hair. In addition to increased hair growth, porphyria has several other manifestations in common with the werewolf myth. People who suffer from this disorder cannot tolerate light; and the flesh under the nails recedes, leaving the hands clawlike. In addition, the skin begins to discolor and causes a progressive deterioration of the nose, ears, eyelids, and fingers; accompanied by the formation of sores. Usually the afflicted person ends up with mental problems from mild hysteria to delirium, along with manic-depressive tendencies.

I'm convinced that the werewolf phenomenon originated from diseases such as porphyria, the intake of ergot-infested grain in the

diet, and the medicinal remedies that were used at the time. The combination of hallucinogenic effects of diet and medicine and the misunderstood (at that time) area of mental illness created individuals who thought they were werewolves—and the Dark Ages contributed to their fantasies with superstition and ignorance.

We used to put mentally ill people in shackles and what they call "snake pits" and give them horrible shock treatments. But these days, the only werewolf you're likely to encounter is someone wearing a fur coat who decides to howl at the full moon!

11
Vampires and Chupacabras

Bram Stoker's Dracula character was based on a real person, Prince Vlad Tepes, who was born in 1431 in what is now Romania. *Tepes* means "impaler," and the good prince was so named because of his penchant for staking his enemies—mostly Turks who were fighting for the spread of the Ottoman Empire. It was also rumored that he ate the flesh and drank the blood of his enemies, many times setting up a special table to do so as he watched his opponents being tortured and killed.

Vlad the Impaler became known as Dracula (or "Son of the Dragon") because he was a knight of the sacred Order of the Dragon, which was a chivalric institution formed to shield Christianity from pagan influences.

Of note here is that the dragon was a pre-Christian symbol for protecting the feminine strength and wisdom that had been threatened to be put aside by a paternal religious Christian society.

What's interesting is the symbolism of the female related to Dracula, in much the same way that the werewolf seems to work off of the cycle of the moon, which regulates tides and blood flow (and the corresponding menstrual cycle). Many individuals also assert that destroying a vampire returns it to *Mother* Earth, the life-giving rejuvenation of all living things.

Anyway, in 1453, Constantinople was taken over by Muslim Turks who were about to convert all of Christianity, when Dracula rose up to defend his homeland. His subjects loved him because he defeated the Turks again and again when they tried to enter into his territory. He died violently in 1476, supposedly by the hand of one of his own men, who was rumored to be a Turkish spy.

In Francis Ford Coppola's film *Bram Stoker's Dracula*, Vlad battles the Turks against overwhelming odds. He is victorious, but is then thwarted by the erroneous news that his great love, Elizabeta, has killed herself because she thinks he's dead. Many, including Francine, feel that Dracula and Elizabeta illustrate the political change from the last vestiges of the feminine principle to the very rigid time of the patriarchal rule, which should have been in concert with each other. Instead, the darkness of that time, which led to Dracula himself living in darkness, became another indicator that we need emotion (female) and intellect (male) in all religions.

In *Vampyric Myths and Christian Symbolism: The Love Story of Bram Stoker's Dracula*, Jeffrey Romanyshyn states, "The myth of Dracula in particular, and of the vampyre in general, has been cast in shadows for centuries. The ultimate source of the shadow is not the vampyre, not the incorrect belief that a vampyre is pure evil and lacks a lightness of being, but the Christian church, which at least played the role of midwife in the vampyre's birth."

When Elizabeta tells the dying Dracula at the end of the movie that their love is stronger than death, this certainly gives us all hope that love, which is ultimately God in all its purity, does overcome darkness in the end.

Before Bram Stoker wrote his book, the vampire myth, in one form or another, went back hundreds of years to Central and Eastern Europe, Asia, and the Americas. Many feel that belief in these "creatures of the night" started with vampire bats, which feed on the blood of livestock and other animals. (One wonders, almost humorously, why mosquitoes didn't become associated with the myth as well, but it's reasonable to say that a bat is far more ominous and mysterious living in dark caves than a pesky insect is.) Throughout history, vampires have been defamed as immortal, blood-sucking entities who take the lives of others by drinking their blood. On one level, this reveals our desire for immortality, but it also comes with a price: wandering the earth until the end of time.

Much has been written about the symbology of the deeper meanings of the vampire and where it stems from. For example, vampires also can't see the light of day, which is interesting because light symbolically represents good; neither can they cross water, which Francine says stems from the fact that water is used to purify, make clean, and even baptize. Here are some other common beliefs about vampires and where they originated:

— The fact that vampires **can't see their reflections** goes back to my Jewish heritage (on my father's side). When someone dies, Jews traditionally drape all the mirrors in their homes. Only later did I find out why this was done: It was believed that people who died would see their reflection and not know they were dead; thus, they would be trapped in the mirror, feeling that they were still alive for all eternity.

— We've also heard that vampires are afraid of **garlic.** In my research, I haven't been able to uncover why garlic was supposedly so repellent to vampires, but I did find a myth that said if you put a rose on a dead person's chest, it kept the soul from wandering. Perhaps the opposite of this would be to place garlic, which has a very pungent odor, on the deceased to repel vampires. (After all, when I was a youngster in school, Grandma Ada—who didn't believe in vampires—hung a bag of garlic around my neck to ward off diphtheria. Needless to say, I didn't get the disease—the bag smelled so bad that no one would come near me.)

In his book *The Vampire in Europe,* Montague Summers wrote that on the eve of St. George's Day in Transylvania, every farmer decorated their gates with bunches of wild rose bushes to keep out evil, witches, and possibly vampires. In addition, it's thought by some that nightshade and wolfsbane (also called "monkshood") were used as "vampire repellers" before garlic because of their poisonous qualities.

— **Wooden stakes** were believed to kill vampires, as were bullets (which may be where the idea of killing werewolves with silver bullets also originated). In the 1885 article "Transylvanian Superstitions," Emily Gerard wrote: ". . . every person killed by a nosferatu [vampire] likewise becomes a vampire after death, and will continue to suck the blood of innocent people till the spirit has been exorcized, either by opening the grave of the person suspected and driving a stake through the corpse, or firing a pistol shot into the coffin." Bram Stoker's notes referred to this passage—no doubt he incorporated its ideas into *Dracula*.

Hawthorn was considered by some people in Eastern and Central Europe to be the best material for a stake to stop a vampire because it had thorns, and thorny bushes (including the rose) were used extensively to protect people from vampires.

There's no way that we can cover everything that's been written about vampires in one chapter, or even one book—Anne Rice has proven that. But I would like to insert here that *they do not exist,* except as an attempt by humankind to explain evil.

Chupacabras

One of the lesser-known mysterious creatures of the world is the chupacabra (which means "goat sucker"), but it's getting more and more attention these days. The reason for this is because the beast kills animals by sucking all their blood, almost like a vampire.

Chupacabras seek out farm animals (generally goats, chickens, and horses), puncture their flesh (usually in the neck), and drain the blood from the bodies—in some cases, removing the internal organs as well. One of the interesting things about chupacabras is that there is little if any blood left around the animals they kill— and except for drained blood and the occasional organ removal, the rest of the bodies of the animals they attack are left intact.

According to **www.crystalinks.com**, the creature has been seen throughout Mexico, the Caribbean, and South America, as well as in the southwestern United States and Florida. An article on the site states:

Chupacabras are described as about four feet tall when standing erect, have huge red elongated eyes, grey skin that is part fur and part feathers, short arms with claws, legs like a kangaroo, and a line of sharp spikes down the middle of its back. They are supposedly very powerful animals. Some report that the chupacabras have wings and can fly.

It's remarkable that there are carved Mayan stones in Palenque, Mexico, that depict a strange creature that's very similar to the drawings made from reported eyewitness sightings of the chupacabra. So it seems that this mysterious animal has actually been with us a long time.

Orange balls of light also seem to show up at the same time as chupacabra sightings, which some have linked to UFOs. Now why would extraterrestrials want animal blood? Because it seems that it's not only hunger that drives them, but also a type of research. When we get to the chapter on alien abductions, you'll see that not everything that comes from outer space is here for good. Yes, they're like us in many ways, but they also have to contend with their own renegade or demented factions. This is why chupacabra sightings seem to diminish for a time, and then we'll hear about a rash of them—the creatures must come back under the control of those who brought them here.

These incidents usually occupy some back page in the newspaper as almost a filler, as do many unexplained sightings. (Even strange occurrences in the sky seem to be reported this way. We always hear it was "swamp fog," "a meteor," "weather balloons" or some other outrageous explanation. I remember in the 1980s in San Jose, California, strange lights were seen over the city, which were put down to flares in swamp fog. First of all, San Jose isn't in a swamp; and second, why didn't they investigate where the flares originated from?)

I believe that the chupacabra is quite different from the vampire bat—it's actually a creature from another planet that was put here for research purposes and sometimes runs amok.

12
Children's Invisible Friends

For years, parents have wondered what to do about their children and their so-called imaginary friends. Kids go so far as to give these pals nicknames, like BoBo or Beaky; or real names, such as Tony or Karen. They will not only talk to them, but may also want to set a place at the table for them. Even my own boys had their "imaginary" pals—Paul had Timothy, and Chris had Charlie—who, by the way, are actually my sons' spirit guides.

Some guides come to children as other kids because it may be easier for these youngsters to accept. Yet children may also have "grown-up friends" to talk to and play with—for example, Francine came to me as a grown woman. I'm sure she did so because companionship, love, and guidance from my own mother were null-and-void—so Francine filled that gap.

Children's eyes are so unclouded by the world that they see the dimension from which the guides come. Yet their invisible friends seem to fade from their reality—I'm convinced that life crowds in and pushes them away, or well-meaning parents tell them that they have an overactive imagination. To encourage our children, we should get them to talk about their friends. In fact, our kids can even give us very psychic messages from their guides.

For example, a little boy named David recently told his mother that Marty (his imaginary friend) said that her dad (David's grandfather) was going home to God's house. David's mother didn't pay much attention until the next day, when she got word that her father had died suddenly of a heart attack. Likewise, Francine told me when I was staying with my grandmother that my grandpa, whom I loved dearly, had gone to heaven—she even gave me the exact time he made the transition.

You don't have to probe, but in a conversational or matter-of-fact way, question your child and act interested. I bet you'll be amazed at the information that comes through. Don't be afraid—if we listen to our children, we'll enhance their communion with their guides and with God and their angels. Then we'll have a group of people who will grow up not feeling so alone, and who realize that God sends emissaries to guide us along the way.

13
Extraterrestrials

Just like many other people, I feel that it's ridiculous to think that our small, insignificant planet—which is on the outside edge of a medium-sized galaxy that contains billions of planets and is among thousands of other galaxies that *also* contain billions of planets—is the only one that contains life. There has to be some kind of ego, ignorance, or "I just don't give a damn" attitude behind such a theory. I'm not condemning any of the above—I just find it incredible that we can't believe that God didn't make other life in His image to inhabit this almost infinite universe we reside in.

"To suppose that earth is the only populated world in infinite space is as absurd as to believe that in an entire field sown with millet, only one grain will grow."
— Metrodorus of Chios, fourth-century B.C. philosopher

Volumes could be written on UFOs and extraterrestrials alone (and, of course, many have), but that's not really my purpose here. I'm just trying to give you explanations about some of the world's mysteries using my God-given ability, doing my best to back it up with facts that are known but not necessarily understood.

In other words, some "facts" still can't be explained, leading to mysteries within mysteries. This isn't new—science continually runs into this in the pursuit of truth, which is why it always tries to go step-by-step. In attempting to solve a mystery, science will many times uncover or discover a new mystery, and on and on it goes. . . .

My Own Experiences

I've researched the subject of extraterrestrials off and on for the last 60 years or so—that's because when I was a little girl, my psychic grandmother would regale me with stories of life on other planets. I'm sure she got a lot of her information from her guides and her own psychic insight, just as I do today.

It's funny that I wasn't a great believer in reincarnation early on, but I had no trouble hearing about how an alien visited Grandma Ada when she was picking tomatoes outside her little house on Monroe Street in Kansas City.

Grandma Ada's Visitor

I had my grandmother tell me this story so many times that she must have wanted to tape my mouth shut, but each time, she told it in the same way without embellishment. Anyway, Grandma Ada was standing in her garden one day when she saw a blinding flash. It was sunny, so she figured that it was a type of ball lightning that often happens in Missouri, or a quirk of her eyesight. As she bent down to pick another tomato, a shadow fell across her. She looked up to see a man dressed in all-silver clothing, which appeared to be made from parachute material, but was stranger looking; and it also seemed to be one piece. (She was an expert seamstress, so I imagine that most people wouldn't have taken that much notice of these details.)

She said that he didn't talk, but he *did* communicate. I didn't understand what she meant, so she told me, "You know how you and I do, and sometimes your dad and you do." (She was referring to the telepathy she and I shared, which to this day some say was unreal. And strangely enough, even though my father wasn't from the same genetic line as Grandma Ada, we had remarkable ESP between us as well.)

"Oh, he mind-talked [which was our word for *telepathy* at the time]," I said. She nodded and told me that it was the clearest she'd ever heard. In this way, the visitor asked her what she was doing, and she explained that she was picking tomatoes. When he wondered what they were for, she said that they were to eat and handed him one. He bit into it, promptly made a face, and dropped it.

I was interested in how the creature looked because my great-uncle, who was psychic and worked in the old Spiritualist camps in Florida, was rabid about UFOs. I still have his scrapbook from 1908 to 1911, in which every article about UFOs was carefully logged. Yet he'd never actually seen one, so I think that even though my grandmother didn't let on, she was pleased that *she* had.

She told me that the alien man was tall. (Now, all the men in my family tree were over 6'3", so I can imagine that Grandma Ada must have meant taller than what was common for us—perhaps close to seven feet.) He was also dark haired with beautiful dark eyes, but he didn't look any different from anyone else. The only unusual thing she noticed was that he seemed to have a film that went over his eyes intermittently like a lizard, but aside from that, he wasn't grotesque or strange looking at all. She said that his hair looked a little synthetic, but she wasn't sure. He had a regular mouth and teeth, but the nose was a little broader, almost like Polynesian features. However, he didn't have the misshapen head and large glassy eyes that have been almost hypnotically propelled into the consciousness of Americans and even people around the world.

As Grandma Ada said later, if aliens looked so grotesquely different, they wouldn't be able to visit our planet undetected. (Here my guide Francine interjects to say that whatever you want to believe is great, but she and all her fellow guides have only seen what are humanlike creatures: Some are tall and some are short; some are dark and some are light; some look Caucasian and some look Asian; and so on. Doesn't it make sense that this is how they blend in with us? After all, they're walking among us, even in politics.)

Over the years, when I saw some of Hollywood's aliens (including the movie *E.T.*), I had to laugh because these oddities would certainly have been scrutinized and probed—at the very least, they would have had their DNA taken by some of our scientists. I mean, it's pretty clear to me that what humankind doesn't understand, we have a tendency to vilify or make into monsters.

Close Encounter in the Desert

Now I'd like to tell you about an experience that my former husband and I (along with six other people) had in Death Valley, California, back in the 1980s. We knew some friends who had talked to Francine and asked her when the next UFO sighting would be. Without hesitation, she told us what night and what area of Death Valley to visit to see it. One of our friends rented a very large RV, and we all packed up and set off for the designated rendezvous. We arrived at dark, even though we were supposed to wait until about midnight. Despite the fact that we were all very apprehensive, the time soon arrived.

Although I could have sworn that we parked on a flat road, when I got out of the RV, I felt like I'd somehow been drugged. Everything seemed to be tipped, as if I were suddenly on an incline, and I became very dizzy—even Francine's voice seemed garbled and far away.

I kept my mouth shut because I know only too well how suggestible people can be, but one by one, I watched each of my friends come out, and they all seemed to have the same experience. Even my husband exclaimed, "We didn't park on a hill—what the hell is going on?" My dear friend Tia said the same thing and that she also felt disjointed and dizzy. Francine then came through to tell me that gravity was being disrupted by the UFOs overhead.

Although the moon and stars were the only things illuminating the dark desert night, I suddenly saw a tall figure appear in silhouette over this small hill. Francine said that each of us should meet "him" one at a time. (I wondered why, but since I was somewhat disoriented, I didn't question her.) So one of the men in our group, whom I'll call "D" and who is now passed over, wanted to go first.

We all stood back and watched D approach—as he did, he kept calling back to see if he'd reached the figure yet. (Apparently we could see the figure but D couldn't.) Almost in unison, we yelled, "He's right next to you on the right!" D called back, "Jesus, I can't see, but I can feel him!" We could see the two of them very close together, and when D came back, he said that they'd communicated telepathically.

I went next, and I *could* see the visitor: He was very tall and looked as if he had a type of helmet on, almost like Darth Vader with a metallic visor. I asked, "Where do you come from?"

"You cannot see it in your telescopes, but my planet, PX41, is beyond the Andromeda galaxy," he said.

"Why did you come here?"

"To see what you have done with your planet."

"You must be very disappointed," I remarked.

"No, I am more confused at what you people do to each other."

"Where's your ship?"

"Right above you," he said.

I couldn't see anything and told him so. He said, "We have a device that hides our ship. Because of our speed and a type of shield, we are not detected on your very primitive radars."

"Why did you come to us?" I queried.

"Maybe someday you will write that we are not here to hurt your planet, but rather to observe and help," he responded.

Oh, I thought, somewhat skeptically, *sure I will—as much as I've already revealed what's out of the norm, I'm not going to put my name on that line.* It's not that I didn't believe, but I already talked to spirits, did readings, and started a church . . . now UFOs?

He read my thoughts and said, "You will" (and so I have).

As we came back together, every person in the group had a different story. Each encounter had been profound, and we all felt energized and comforted at the same time. As we stood by the RV, we noticed that a huge streak had appeared in the sky, which quickly vanished.

The coyotes that were so still now began to let out a crescendo of noise that I've never heard before. They seemed to be surrounding us, so we quickly realized that we should get back in the RV.

Once inside, nobody spoke for a long time, as we were all lost in our own thoughts. When we did finally come out of our reverie, all of us had the same feelings and visuals, but each had received a different message. We called the alien "Mr. X," and to this day I'm not sure if anybody else in the group has ever talked about it. It was such a profound experience—one that's as real to me today as it was then.

John

Mr. X wasn't the first extraterrestrial I ever encountered—that honor goes to the alien I met in the 1970s in Palo Alto, California, a suburban town near Stanford University. My sister and I were eating at a place called L'Omelette, which we liked to go to after we got off from work at St. Albert the Great, a Catholic elementary school. We were studying our menus when a young man asked if he could join us. Even though I was married, my sister wasn't, and the man seemed sweet and shy; besides, there were a lot of people around, so we said okay.

The minute he sat down, an alarm went off inside me. It wasn't as if I felt that he was a rapist or a killer—instead, I just got no reading, which is impossible for me. I'm not trying to be egotistical, but everyone who comes near me gives me *something*. This guy was a blank.

Francine told me, "He's not from here," and I knew he wasn't a ghost because at least they have a history. When I asked his name, he paused and said, "John," almost as if he had to think about it.

The television over the bar at the end of the eating area was showing a baseball game, and our new friend seemed to be fascinated by it. Finally, he asked me what they were doing.

I said, "It's called baseball." My sister gave me this "What the hell?" look, and I promptly kicked her under the table.

"Why do they do that?" John wondered aloud.

I told him that it was a game, but he shook his head in confusion. It was then that I noticed his hair, which looked like a doll's, put in one piece at a time. (Now please remember that this was in the '70s, long before hair plugs and transplants were commonplace.)

"Would you like something to eat?" I asked him after a bit.

He said, "I guess so. . . . What are you going to have?"

"Fish, salad, and Jell-O."

"Me, too," he replied, seeming elated that he didn't have to make a decision.

My sister was silent, giving me sidelong looks, but she's been with me all her life and trusts what I do. She was also aware that I knew the owner of this restaurant, so if we were in danger, I wouldn't have any problem going to get him.

When the food came, that's when it became pathetically comical, and I emphasize *pathetic*. John didn't know what to do, so I showed him the fork—and he stared at it. He took a bite of his fish and asked what it was. I told him that it comes out of the ocean, and he made a face and summarily put down his fork. He did drink water and seemed to be fascinated with the salt. I showed him how to put it in his hand, and he licked that ferociously. The topper was when he tried to drink the Jell-O.

"John," I said, "where do you live?"

"Oh, here, there, and everywhere," he responded.

"Why did you happen to come here?" I asked.

"I was just looking around," he replied. "I have been walking around the school," which I assumed meant Stanford.

My sister and I were getting ready to go, but I kept watching him and his sheer inquisitiveness at everything going on around him. We got outside, with John in tow like a puppy dog, and my sister took out her comb.

He asked, "What is that?"

That did it. I said, "John, you can trust us. Where are you from and why are you here?"

He looked me square in the face and said, "Someday you will know who I am and who *we* are." Then he repeated Mr. X's words: "We are observing and trying to help." Then he gave me his telephone number and said, "If you need to contact me, call me and we will talk more." He even gave me an address along with his number. As I watched him walk away, he kind of shuffled, almost as if he wasn't sure of our gravity. (John Keel, author of *The Mothman Prophecies,* has noted that aliens tend to do this.)

Well, needless to say, the phone number was wrong, and no one at that address had ever heard of John. And I wasn't surprised a bit.

Part III

Unexplained Objects

Two views of the crystal skull ShaNaRa (courtesy of Nick Nocerino).

14
The Crystal
Skulls

Archaeologists seem to disagree on where 13 skulls made entirely out of crystal, which have been found from Mexico to Peru, originated from. However, Francine says that even in her day (A.D. 1500), the crystal skulls were known to the Aztec, Incan, and Mayan cultures. This information goes along with what a wonderful Website, **www.world-mysteries.com**, says: that the skulls are anywhere from 5,000 to 36,000 years old.

Even the most accomplished crystal and glass blowers don't know how these treasures were made or how they've survived, but they do resemble human skulls— several, such as the celebrated Mitchell-Hedges Skull, even include a removable jawbone. This famous artifact was pur-portedly found in 1924 by F. A. Mitchell-Hedges, who claimed that his daughter, Anna, had discovered it. There doesn't seem to be any proof of this; in fact, the British Museum maintains that it has records of Mitchell-Hedges bidding for the skull at an auc-tion at Sothebys in London in 1943, and this has been verified.

There are those who say that F. A. Mitchell-Hedges had the skull made to finance his various expeditions. This speculation is partly based on the nebulous history of the skull and that, even though it's been shown to the public more than any other of the skulls, Anna Mitchell-Hedges won't allow it to be tested further. I'm sure it doesn't matter: Whether this skull was discovered in an ancient Mayan ruin or a temple in Belize—or if Anna was even at the site where it was found—doesn't take away from the mag-nificence of the prize.

The Mitchell-Hedges Skull is made of clear quartz crystal, and both the cranium and the mandible came from the same block. (Whether it's a female or male skull is open to debate, but judging by the size, high cheekbones, and more fragile demeanor, I'd say that it was a female.) And even though the skull has been through a battery of tests, no one can figure out how it was carved. It was done so against the grain, which baffles scientists who insist that this would have shattered the crystal. Several of the skulls were also tested for microscopic scratches and none were found, which would indicate that they weren't carved with today's metal instruments and technology.

Art restorer Frank Dorland oversaw testing of the Mitchell-Hedges Skull at the Hewlett-Packard Laboratories in 1970, and his best hypothesis for the making of the skull was that it was roughly chiseled out with diamonds, and then a silicon sand-and-water

solution was used to smooth it—and it was estimated that this process would have required up to *300 years* for human hands to complete.

My spirit guide Francine told me that the crystal skulls came from a very explicit mold, which was made out of a substance close to our titanium. The quartz was heated in some way, poured into the mold, and then gently cooled. At that point, 15, not 13, skulls were sent to different parts of the Andes; through migration and war, they then became scattered across Latin America.

Aside from the Mitchell-Hedges Skull, others that have been recovered include the Aztec Skull; the Amethyst Skull; the Paris Crystal Skull; the Texas Skull, also called "Max"; the ET Skull, named because of its pointed cranium and exaggerated overbite, which makes it looks like an alien skull (however, humans' heads come in all shapes and sizes, so don't immediately jump to the conclusion that it really is an alien skull); the Mayan Crystal Skull; the Rose Quartz Skull, which is larger and similarly carved like the Mitchell-Hedges Skull; the Rainbow Skull; the Jesuit Skull; the Agate Chip Skull; and the Sha-Na-Ra Skull (which I'll discuss in a little bit). There are other crystal skulls out there, but many have been determined to be recently made and are therefore not classified as part of the original ancient 13.

Interestingly, the Aztec Skull is no longer displayed at the Museum of Man in London—and museum personnel and visitors claim to have seen it move on its own within its protective case. Francine says that this is because crystal is an energy conductor that moves toward the highest degree of electrical emanations. In other words, people with kinetic energy (which manifests itself by moving objects) would be prime targets to move the skull. (I'll talk more about kinetic energy later in the book.)

Francine says that, as with the stones of Egypt's pyramids, we don't yet possess the technology to tap in to the knowledge that was put in the crystal skulls. Since crystal has always been a conductor (after all, the first radios were old crystal sets), much ancient information was put into the skulls. Francine also says that these artifacts were made by her ancestors—who were very adept at carving and polishing with a white, powdery sand—and they were apparently religious symbols that dated back thousands of years before her birth. These symbols showed Francine's people two things: (1) Life is fleeting; and (2) we should always honor and remember the dead we'll someday join.

It's interesting to note that Mexican communities still revere their dead, celebrating their ancestors on the *Día de los Muertos* ("Day of the Dead"). Francine also states that in the last ten years, people have tried to duplicate the skulls, which has shed doubt on the true 13 skulls that exist today.

I was also reminded that Francine once told me that all the world's pyramids carried crystals on their apexes because they brought knowledge from the ancients. Even today, we wear crystals because they absorb negativity. And an old Native American tradition that's been passed down through the ages claims that when we lose our negativity and our shortsighted minds, crystals can be used as instruments for seeing evil things and warding them off, as well as for healing the sick. Are they trying to tell us that crystals can heal? Yes. Are the artifacts telepathic? Yes.

There's no doubt that the crystal skulls (at least the authentic ones) have healing powers or properties, for countless people have felt their beneficial effects. I believe that this is thanks to the skulls' generation of energy, combined with electricity and God's hand.

In fact, one of the most amazing parts of crystal-skull research is that it has given many psychics accurate information on past events such as Atlantis, as well as on future occurrences—it's not any different from scrying (looking in water) or crystal-ball gazing. I've never been one for props, but here you're using something that holds a cell memory like our own bodies, so why not try to tap in to it?

I remember when I experienced the power of a crystal skull myself. In the late 1980s, I was fortunate enough to see an exhibit of artifacts and "mystical treasures" when I ran into my old trusted friend, the great paranormal investigator Nick Nocerino. Nick has accompanied me many times during my investigations of haunted sites, and as luck would have it, he possessed the Sha-Na-Ra Skull (pictured at the beginning of this chapter).

The clear artifact gave off such brilliant prisms of light that I asked to touch it. Nick told me that he didn't ordinarily let anyone handle the skull because people often had weird reactions to it—even days later, some still reported strange dreams and energy that they couldn't explain—but since I was Sylvia . . .

I held the skull, not expecting a darn thing, but its electricity shot through me with such force that I was almost overwhelmed. It wasn't as if I haven't dealt with electrical current before (after all, ghosts have it, which is why they're able to transmit heat and light on infrared film). But this was different. It was similar to a ripple effect, almost like when you're sitting in one of those massage chairs and you feel its pulsations going through you.

I won't forget my encounter with the Sha-Na-Ra Skull—I felt so good after I touched it; and I was also incredibly proud of my friend Nick, who had a real skull and who had also helped find the excavation site where it and the Rainbow Skull were discovered.

If you get the chance, try to touch a crystal skull. Whether it's ancient or new, you'll still feel an electrical charge. Just imagine: If you could learn from the skulls, rather than having someone tell you about them, you could personally experience this upward thrust of increased intuition and healing.

Note from Sylvia: It's interesting to note that the 1938 discovery of stone discs in China, which purportedly have been decoded, tell of another extraterrestrial visitation by a people known as "the Dropa" (whom I previously mentioned in Chapter 3). The Dropa left information on stone discs that recount their story. They're similar to the crystal skulls in that they're also mysterious storehouses of knowledge beyond our current civilization. In fact, 22 more crystal skulls (know as the Beijing skulls) were found in the caves in which several of these discs were located. In all, 716 discs have been found to date, but due to the secrecy of the Chinese government, not much is known of these treasures.

15
The Ica Stones

Just north of the Pampa Colorada in Peru lies the coastal farming community of Ica, home to a physician named Javier Cabrera, who was directly descended from the town's Spanish founder. In 1966, an illiterate farmer gave Dr. Cabrera a stone for his birthday that had an image of a fish carved on it. Dr. Cabrera noticed that the fish seemed odd; upon researching it, he discovered that the carving on the stone matched a specimen that was supposed to have been extinct for thousands of years.

Dr. Cabrera questioned his friend about where the stone had come from, but the farmer said that he'd found it in a cave, in which more treasures could be found. The good doctor then said that he'd buy any of the stones that the farmer could find. The farmer already had a reputation of hawking them to tourists, so he had no problem getting more to sell to his friend. Dr. Cabrera ended up with more than 11,000 stones in his collection, and estimated that over 100,000 like them were in existence.

Word of the stones and the farmer got out, so the BBC did a documentary on the phenomenon. It was about this time that the Peruvian government stepped in, diligently questioning the farmer about the origin of the stones. He was told that he'd go to jail for selling the rocks (Peru does have tough antiquity laws), so he quickly changed his story from finding the stones in caves and riverbeds to carving them himself to sell to tourists.

Since the Peruvian government wanted to get rid of any controversy, they accepted the farmer's revised story; to them, the stones were no longer an issue for concern. In addition, the BBC was soundly criticized for airing a story that was obviously a hoax, so they quickly tried to sweep it under the rug. And under the rug was where it might have stayed had it not been for Dr. Cabrera.

A small stone that was meant as a present turned into a lifetime passion for the physician, and he understood that his farmer friend had changed his story to keep from being imprisoned. But what also intrigued Dr. Cabrera was that the stones he'd collected had carvings that depicted such fascinating images and stories that he knew an illiterate farmer could never know of or even imagine them.

So for the last 30 or so years of his life, that Peruvian doctor researched and investigated not only the origin but also the content of the stones, and he desperately tried to get the scientific community to join in. However, he was met with resistance— the "hoax stigma" attached to the stones had made them almost anathema as far as serious scientific study was concerned.

No matter what, Dr. Cabrera would not give up on the stones—he even opened a museum so that people could view his collection. He became an avid amateur archaeologist and geologist in addition to his normal physician duties, and came up with some astounding information and theories regarding these enigmatic rocks (some of which we'll explore a little later on). For now, let's look at the stones themselves and what they depict.

The Ica Stones are made up of a local river rock that's a form of andesite—a hard, gray-to-black volcanic mineral—and they're covered with a layer of natural oxidation (or varnish) that confirms that they are quite old. German laboratories have authenticated that the carvings on the stones are indeed very ancient, and that they have that patina of oxidation over them. (It's well known that locals do carve rocks to sell to tourists in the area, but the incisions in the newly created carvings don't have the oxidation patina on them that the "real" Ica Stones do.) Ranging in size from those that fit in the palm of the hand to those that are as large as two basketballs, all the stones have images or drawings etched into them—and this is where the controversy begins.

Dr. Cabrera's collection is categorized by subject matter that includes humans, ancient animals, lost continents, and the knowledge of global catastrophes. His stones depict pictures of natives adorned with crowns and robes doing medical procedures on patients—there are images of brain transplants; heart transplants; heart surgery, showing blood vessels and arteries being reconnected via reabsorption tubes (which utilizes the natural regeneration of cells); cesarean sections, with acupuncture as anesthesia; transplant surgery, employing procedures that are just now being used by modern medicine; artificial life-support systems, using energy that seems to be conveyed by the surgeons themselves; and work with genetic codes.

There are other images of maps showing Earth from an aerial view, with several unfamiliar land masses and a completely different continent configuration. When scientists compared these maps to computer simulations, they were found to be highly accurate images of what our planet would have looked like 13 million years ago. (These maps also clearly show the continents of Atlantis and Lemuria.)

There are other drawings of men using telescopes to observe planets, comets, and star systems; and several stones depict men

riding dinosaurs—both on land and in the air! The art on the rocks is amazingly accurate in almost every way. For example, the dinosaurs shown are known to have existed, the medical images are accurate and in surprising detail, and the stars and planets are correct in their locations.

Who made these stones? Where did they come from? The farmer's story of finding them in a cave that was uncovered because of local flooding now seems plausible—but where are the remaining stones hidden now, and for what reason?

After studying the Ica Stones for years and consulting with various geologists and scientists, Dr. Cabrera had his theories. He postulated that a very ancient civilization, which was originally from a star system in the Pleiades, landed on Earth and attempted to colonize it. He also claimed that at that time, this planet was entirely different from the one we live on today. It was comprised of an 80 percent land mass with very little water, and because of the planetary conditions, the atmosphere had heated up considerably. Therefore, he theorized, this ancient civilization tried to manipulate the biological cycles of nature to correct the situation, but the attempted corrections caused massive tectonic shifts, great floods, and the movement of continents (in other words, cataclysmic events that changed the planet's land masses). With Earth's stability in question, this ancient civilization prepared to depart for their home planet in the Pleiades. (A large stone in Cabrera's library shows the hemispheres of that planet having intelligent life and space-traveling capability.)

Dr. Cabrera also believed that the Pampa Colorada was their "spaceport," so to speak, and that these visitors used a form of electromagnetic energy to propel their ships—in fact, several etchings in his collection show ships suspended in an electromagnetic cushion whose field is controlled by both the surface of the planet itself and the craft. Since the Pampa Colorada has huge deposits of iron ore, he surmised that this area had an electro-magnetic field of extraordinary strength.

Many who knew Dr. Cabrera were convinced of his sincer-ity and honesty, and he was considered to be a kind and dedicated individual who had a passion for the Ica Stones and for decod-ing them. It was also rumored for many years that he had a secret chamber of stones in his museum that he never let the public see. These special rocks held a "message for humankind" that Dr. Cabrera insisted would be let out someday when we were ready.

Francine says that her people knew of the stones in the early 1500s and that they were considered sacred. She goes on to state that the stones were indeed a record left behind by extraterres-trials who inhabited the area millions of years ago and whose effect also extended to Pampa Colorada and the surrounding areas. They also had an impact on very early cultures in not only Peru, but in Atlantis and Lemuria as well, which influenced other highly advanced later civilizations such as the Egyptians. Francine also told me that in about 15 years, humans will be able to tap in to these stones for the information contained therein, which she said functions like computer databases.

Dr. Cabrera was ostracized for his theories and his fascina-tion with the Ica Stones. Nevertheless, he persevered despite crit-icism and the onslaught of skeptics throughout much of his life, eventually dying of cancer in December 2001. To the doubters who pointed out that the farmer admitted to carving the stones himself, Dr. Cabrera said that if that had been the case, his friend would not only have had to know the inner workings of advanced medical techniques, but he would have also had to

possess intricate knowledge of the stars, planets, spaceships, dinosaurs, and the like . . . as well as having to average carving a stone a day, seven days a week, for more than 40 years—all of which seemed highly unlikely for an illiterate farmer.

Skeptics can't explain how the farmer could carve more than 15,000 stones (other than to say that he'd had help), nor can they justify why an ignorant laborer would go to the trouble of doing all this just to sell rocks to tourists. Cynics also can't account for those maps of ancient origin, which show how Earth looked in earlier days as confirmed by geologists using computer simulation. In other words, the Ica Stones still remain a mystery that no one can explain with any sort of incontrovertible proof—which, of course, is why they're still a mystery.

Photograph of Piri Reis Map courtesy of
© Adventures Unlimited Press, *Maps of the
Ancient Sea Kings* by Charles Hapgood.

16
Otherworldly Maps and Instruments

It seems that the more we research the mysteries of this planet, the more we discover an intelligence that's beyond anything we know—a center point seems to direct us beyond Earth to another group of entities who had a hand in planning our progress. The three examples in this chapter will illustrate what I mean.

The Piri Reis Map

While researching this book, I came across an interesting article on **www.world-mysteries.com** that stated:

> In 1929, a group of historians found an amazing map drawn on a gazelle skin. Research showed that it was a genuine document drawn in 1513 by Piri Reis, a famous admiral of the Turkish fleet in the sixteenth century. His passion was cartography. His high rank within the Turkish navy allowed him to have a privileged access to the Imperial Library of Constantinople. The Turkish admiral admits in a series of notes on the map that he compiled and copied the data from a large number of source maps, some of which dated back to the fourth century B.C. or earlier.

It turns out that this old chart, which scientists who have studied it call the "Piri Reis Map," has raised quite a controversy. The mystery stems from what the map contains, namely the northern coastline of Antarctica in detail, along with the western coast of Africa and the eastern coast of South America. Now how was the perfectly detailed and *accurate* coastline of Antarctica drawn 300 years before it was discovered? And perhaps even more puzzling—how does the map show the coastline of Antarctica under ice? (Think about this for a moment: The map is so accurate that modern-day scientists could use it to update their own charts!)

Many scientists say that the absolute earliest date that the continent of Antarctica wasn't covered with ice was 4000 B.C., while others put it even further back in time (a million years or so). Now couple that with the fact that scientists say that the earliest civilizations began in 3000 to 4000 B.C.—and these individuals certainly didn't have the technology to map with such accuracy—and you get a mystery that can't be explained. Let's examine this a bit closer.

In the preface of his book *Maps of the Ancient Sea Kings* (Adventures Unlimited Press, 1997), Charles H. Hapgood states:

> In one field, ancient sea charts, it appears that accurate information has been passed down from people to people. It appears that the charts must have originated with a people unknown; that they were passed on, perhaps by the Minoans (the Sea Kings of ancient Crete) and the Phoenicians, who were for a thousand years and more the greatest sailors of the ancient world. We have evidence that they were collected and studied in the great library of Alexandria [Egypt] and the compilations of them were made by the geographers who worked there.

Professor Hapgood asked the U.S. Air Force to evaluate the Piri Reis Map and got this response:

> 6 July 1960
> Subject: Admiral Piri Reis Map
> To: Prof. Charles H. Hapgood
> Keene College
> Keene, New Hampshire
>
> Dear Professor Hapgood,
>
> Your request of evaluation of certain unusual features of the Piri Reis map of 1513 by this organization has been reviewed.

The claim that the lower part of the map portrays the Princess Martha Coast of Queen Maud Land, Antarctic, and the Palmer Peninsular, is reasonable. We find that this is the most logical and in all probability the correct interpretation of the map. The geographical detail shown in the lower part of the map agrees very remarkably with the results of the seismic profile made across the top of the ice-cap by the Swedish-British Antarctic Expedition of 1949.

This indicates the coastline had been mapped before it was covered by the ice-cap. The ice-cap in this region is now about a mile thick.

We have no idea how the data on this map can be reconciled with the supposed state of geographical knowledge in 1513.

Harold Z. Ohlmeyer, Lt. Colonel, USAF Commander

Hapgood hypothesizes that Piri Reis probably came into possession of some of the ancient charts that were either copied or transferred to the library at Constantinople and used them in drawing his map. But where did the original charts come from? Hapgood and others theorize that a highly advanced civilization made them, using technology that was far superior to what was possessed by humankind until the last half of the 18th century (because spheroid trigonometry wasn't understood until then).

In 1953, a Turkish naval officer sent the Piri Reis Map to be studied by the U.S. Navy Hydrographic Bureau, which solicited the help of Arlington H. Mallery, an authority on ancient maps. After a considerable study, Mallery found that the only way for the Piri Reis Map to be so accurate was through aerial surveying (bet you never thought I was going to get around to tying this in to UFOs, did you?). Now, who had the capacity to do an aerial surveillance 6,000 years ago?

Francine, as well as my own psychic ability, tells me that the map was actually drawn about *12,000* years ago by extraterrestrials from the Andromeda galaxy, who then gave it to the Atlanteans. From there, it ended up in the library at Alexandria, and copies were transferred before it was burned down.

Now here's another surprise: The Piri Reis Map isn't the only one to have used these ancient alien schematics; instead, it seems that charts were made all over the earth at a very ancient time with uncanny precision. For example, maps have been discovered from the 14th century that show Greenland under its thick ice cap; others show a land strip that joins Alaska and Siberia, which has been covered by water since the end of the glacial period; and a cartographic document copied from an older source and carved on a rock column in China was found to date back to A.D. 1137.

All these documents boast an accuracy that couldn't have been done at the time that they were drawn, since all appear to have used spheroid trigonometry. Scholars now think that an ancient map of the entire Earth was done and that these other maps are just segments of that alien cartography.

Nazca Lines

Down in Peru is the Pampa Colorada, which means "Colored Plain" or "Red Plain," and it's home to another mystery (along with the Ica Stones, which we discussed in the last chapter). In this desert region are more than 300 lines and figures, including some in the shapes of plants and animals. They were made by removing rock from the plateau and exposing the lighter-colored earth underneath. They were created with obvious care, but here's the kicker: You can only distinguish these images from the air!

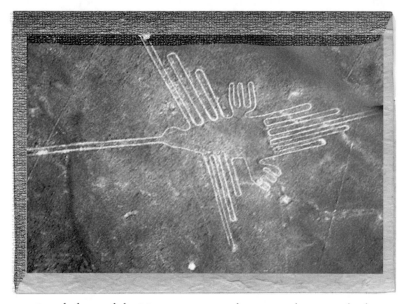

Aerial photo of the Nazca pictogram depicting a hummingbird.

Scientists say that an ancient people called the *Nazca* built these lines, but no one knows why or how they did it with such precision. There are straight lines that run for miles, crisscrossing the plains, in the shape of birds, triangles, spirals, rectangles, wavy lines, and so on. This myriad collection of markings covers hundreds of acres, and some lines even seem to have been traveled like "roads" by large groups of people. Researchers wonder if these are ancient gods, patterns of constellations, star pointers, or even a gigantic map. Some even speculate that one of the figures, a giant spider, is actually a representation of the constellation Orion.

The Nazca civilization is pre-Incan, yet the lines are a complicated, multisided pictogram. Francine said that it's also not without whimsy, in the same way that a graphic artist would create on a computer screen. She said that the lines and geometric configurations are much like crop circles (which I'll discuss in a bit): astrological road maps to the star or galaxy from which these visitors came.

Along the Pacific coast is a giant trident or candelabra pointing toward the Pampa Colorada; farther south is a mountain called Sierra Pintada, which is also covered in pictograms. These sites weren't just guideposts—they were also made to show that there is a supreme being, a real creative force that oversees everything on this planet, which comes from other star systems. In addition, about 850 miles south of the Pampa Colorada is a pictogram of the largest human figure in the world, dressed in what looks like a spacesuit. Called the "Giant of Atacama," it stands around 390 feet tall and has lines similar to the Nazca surrounding it. The Giant is a depiction of the so-called commander of this mission to Earth . . . just as we left our footsteps and flag on the moon.

Pictorial histories have also been discovered in cave drawings around the world. Other pictures, such as those in the ancient tombs of Egypt, show everyday life in that time period. Whether it was fighting or farming, our ancient astronaut ancestors wanted to leave us a record of what life was like. I don't think that's any different from burying a time capsule for future generations to uncover. Like the Incas and Mayans and especially the

Egyptians, our neighbors from space left us a picture book—one that we still argue about, even though it's glaringly simple.

We have pyramids, crop circles, Nazca lines, ancient Sanskrit texts that tell of flying machines and devastating weapons, the Roswell incident, Area 51, thousands of UFO photos, stories of abductions, the Piri Reis Map, and a plethora of other artifacts, carvings, and archaeological discoveries too numerous to mention—I don't know how much more we need as proof to convince us that we're not alone. Why is it so "mystical" to believe that we were aided by residents of another planet who helped us get started and still come back to check on us?

The Antikythera Mechanism

In 1900, Greek divers found the wreck of a ship off the island of Antikythera at a depth of about 150 feet. They recovered statues, pottery, and jewelry, but as it turns out, a few corroded green lumps with a gearlike mechanism inside was the greatest find of all. The "Antikythera mechanism," as it's called by scientists, was found on a ship that was dated to around 87 B.C. This would make the Antikythera mechanism at least 2,000 years old—what's even more astonishing is that to date, it's the most complex mechanism that old that has ever been found.

At first, the mechanism appeared to be a clocklike machine, but upon further examination, it was found to contain at least 20 different gears that interacted with each other in such a way that it could calculate the motion of the planets, sun, and moon. Derek Price, the late science historian at Yale University, was one of the first to study the device at any length, and he concluded that nothing like this instrument has been preserved elsewhere; in fact, nothing comparable to it was even alluded to in any ancient scientific text or literature. Price went on to state that from what's known of science in the Hellenistic Age, the device shouldn't even exist.

Much of the written material that we've discovered from the ancient Greeks has shown that they had great philosophical expertise and mathematical genius, but even the most complex mechanical devices described by age-old Greek writers such as Hero of Alexandria and Vitruvius contained only basic gearing. The Greeks utilized that knowledge of gears for relatively simple projects such as water-driven mills or taximeters (which measured the distance a carriage traveled—much like our modern odometers).

It wasn't known until the Antikythera mechanism was discovered that the Greeks actually had knowledge of and used a more complex gear technology. According to many reports, the mechanism had many dials and at least 20 gears; and instructions in Greek found inscribed on its box told how the instrument functioned. There are numerous inscriptions on the gears, some of which were numbered to show how the gears were located, along with how to reconstruct the mechanism.

As the instrument was cleaned, scientists were able to take a closer look at what it was and how it was put together—and they realized that the device was more complex than first realized. Derek Price had concluded from his study that the Antikythera mechanism was used to predict the position of the sun and moon on any given date; new scientific study concluded that he was correct, but his explanation didn't go far enough.

Evidently, an input apparatus such as an axle or turnstile handle connects to a crown gear that controls the functions of the other gears in the mechanism, reversing gears where necessary to get the desired calculations. Dials on the outside of the enclosing box show the zodiac; the sun and the moon; and the five planets of Mercury, Venus, Mars, Saturn, and Jupiter. It was basically an astronomical calendar computer: The gears turned annually to indicate the different positions of the planets, moon, and sun in the months and days of the year. The Greeks possibly used this device for navigation, festivals, planting times, or just pure scientific knowledge; and it was the forerunner of the clocks and watches of today.

Mr. McBride, one of my college professors, liked to say, "Girls, there is nothing new under the sun" . . . and the more I research, the more I find this to be true. There's even historical data preserved in Oxford that shows that there's a 13th-century Islamic geared calendar computer that tells the cycles of the sun and moon; however, nothing seems to be as sophisticated as the Antikythera mechanism. I believe that this is because the device was also a product of the Andromeda aliens. Human beings simply did not have the resources or the wherewithal to create all those gears that were necessary to tell where the planets were. Yet a higher intelligence that wasn't of this world could—and did.

17
The Pyramids and the Sphinx

I've been to Egypt about ten times with my former husband, but many of these trips were also with hundreds of people who can validate what I've said there (and what I will say here).

Before we go any further, however, I'd like to tell you a story about something that happened about 30 years ago. It's more important than anyone can realize, because what came out of this one episode set me on a path that even I, psychically, could never have imagined the far-reaching effects of.

At the time I was doing readings for people, but I was also performing hypnosis on clients with addictions.

(I'd studied with Dr. Royal at the University of Kansas City and had also taken hypnosis courses from Gil Boynes, a noted instructor.) I was in my little office in Campbell, California, when a client came in for hypnosis for weight reduction. I started to put him under, when all of a sudden he "flipped" on me, which in hypnosis terms means that he was going to do what he wanted and go where he wanted. Being patient, I thought, *I'll listen, and then I'll bring him back to the weight programming.*

My client began to speak in a strange voice with an odd-sounding dialect. I said, "Please talk in English—I don't understand what you're saying." He did, but at first I still didn't know what he was talking about. He said things like, "They're so silly—they don't know how we got those huge rocks to sit perfectly and symmetrically on top of each other."

I finally asked, "Where are you?" and he sounded almost aggravated when he replied, "I'm in Egypt."

Oh great! I thought. Grandma Ada, who was an accomplished psychic, believed in past lives, but at that time I was on the fence. I felt that we had more than likely lived before, but the here-and-now was more my forte. However, I was intrigued, so I asked my client if he was watching what was going on and how it was done.

He immediately came back with, "We used antigravity rods from the large spaceships, which would then leave—and in seconds we'd have a stone that was instantly placed on top of another." He also kept saying that the stones contained imprints of knowledge, much like a library.

When I brought my client out of hypnosis, I asked him if I could keep his tape for a week—something I never do—and he said, "Sure." The next day I took it to a professor of ancient linguistics at Stanford University. As I dropped it off, I thought, *Oh well, I've been called crazy before.*

The next day, I got a call from a Dr. Schmidt, who asked me, "Where did you get this?" When I told him, he said, "I can assure you that this man is speaking in a very ancient dialect." The hair stood up on the back of my neck. How could my client—a young, blond-haired, blue-eyed construction worker who just wanted to lose some weight—possibly know an ancient dialect? Nothing in his genes or in his life would have given rise to this knowledge.

After that episode, whenever I got anyone who flipped and went to a life in Egypt, I'd ask if they knew about the pyramids. Without fail, they all came up with the exact same story—that these cylindrical objects would use a rod to move the stones into place. I became convinced that there's at least a grain of truth here when people from different cultures, times, and genders started telling me the same thing.

All this, of course, led me to the path of past-life regressions, which has been addressed in my book *Past Lives, Future Healing.* I've become a true believer in past lives because it makes perfect sense to me that God gives us more than one or two chances to perfect ourselves for Him.

The Great Pyramid

I didn't get to visit Egypt myself until 1983, and the first thing I noticed was that the country teems with spirituality, which the pyramids especially represent. I love one of the oldest, the Step Pyramid at Saqqara, but nothing compares to the Great Pyramid of Cheops (or Khufu, as it's sometimes called) on the Giza plateau.

The Great Pyramid itself is generally believed to be 4,500 years old, although some claim it may actually be 10,000 years

Here I am at the Pyramids.

old—it depends upon which scientist you listen to. (My spirit guide Francine says that watermarks will show that it was constructed closer to 12,000 to 15,000 years ago.) There's even a theory about the pyramids at Giza being aligned just like the "belt" in the Orion constellation—in fact, mathematical calculations prove that about 10,000 to 12,000 B.C was the period when the pyramids aligned perfectly with that constellation.

When you bask in the shadow of the Great Pyramid, it literally takes your breath away. As I stood there for the first time more than 20 years ago, I was dumbstruck—and I became absolutely convinced that not even thousands of workers toiling over their entire lifetimes could have cut, hauled, and placed those stones by themselves. In order for the Great Pyramid to have been built as Egyptologists say it was, the stones, which weigh an average of 2.5 tons each, would have to have been placed at the rate of one every 45 seconds, which is just not possible.

Scientists have tried to x-ray (for lack of a better word) the Great Pyramid with sound, and each time they get a different reading. Francine says that knowledge put there by an intelligence greater than ours is trapped inside the stones, and it will be revealed in the not-too-distant future. A very close friend of mine, Dr. Zahi Hawass (whom I mentioned earlier), says that he doesn't agree with me, but we love each other anyway. My opinion is that if he *did* agree with me, his position as Egypt's Secretary General of the Supreme Council of Antiquities might be in jeopardy. I, on the other hand, have never been daunted by flying in the face of organized science, religion, philosophy, or what have you. Everything I say I *know* with all my heart and soul, and I only ask others to listen and believe what they wish.

After gazing at the Great Pyramid for quite a while that first time, I decided to go inside, and it was as hot as an oven in there. As I began to ascend the great hall's steps (which go straight up), I was sweating and almost ready to curse myself for being so stupid as to put myself through this—especially since I was in the middle of menopause and felt hot enough most of the time! Although I was having a pity party for myself, I happened to look at the walls that lined the Grand Gallery staircase when, to my surprise, pictures as clear as day began to form. I'm convinced that these images used to be there because even in the dim light, I could detect their faint outline. It's just like when you're preparing to paint and don't realize how dirty your walls are until you take something off them.

The pictures took form: Each one depicted, in beautiful color, a birth, a pubescent youth, what looked like marriage vows, a family standing together, a group working in a field or sitting in a circle together, a person standing in prayer (it looked like Isis), an old man with a stick to help him walk, and a sarcophagus.

Oh my God, I thought, *this isn't really a tomb—it's a symbol of man's ascent through his lifetime!* This logically explains why they never found any mummies buried in the King's or Queen's Chamber. It also reminded me of the ancient riddle of the Sphinx: What walks on four legs in the morning, two legs in the afternoon, and three legs at night? The answer, of course, is the human. A baby crawls on all fours, a young person walks on two legs, and an elderly person uses a cane.

As the group I was with ascended higher, we came to a place where the ceiling was so low that it was like a crawl space. After bending down and getting through, we emerged in the King's Chamber, where only an open sarcophagus stared at us. *Rebirth,* I realized. *The open sarcophagus symbolizes rebirth. We climb through life, through good times and bad; keep on going, no matter how difficult it gets; and then are reborn until our final death here on Earth—at which point, we're released to go to the Other Side. This is a real temple of worship and knowledge,* I thought, and Francine said, "Very good! Now you're getting it."

She's just lucky I love her . . . sometimes there seems to be a bit of condescension and sarcasm in her tone (of course I know it's just the way I take it). I don't often feel this way, but being hot and tired and sweating profusely, I was in no mood for levity. "It's easy for you," I shot back. "You're not going through this!"

I descended, suddenly feeling so vibrant and energized—especially after I stayed in the King's Chamber with the sarcophagus, which greatly reverberated with positive psychic energy, thoughts, songs, rituals, and prayers. Later that night, I gave a lecture on my psychic impressions of the place for everyone who came to the Great Pyramid with me, as I have many times since. It was amazing how many others felt and saw what I did (I know this was true because I saw some of them taking notes, which they then shared with me after I finished talking).

Regardless of what you believe, the Great Pyramid is a mystical place, and no one ever comes out feeling the same. After all the trips I've made there, I have a file cabinet full of hundreds of people's accounts of the life-changing experiences they had. Some folks I've taken with me have even been physically healed in the King's Chamber. The first time I went to Egypt, as I mentioned before, I took about 80 people, but on my next trip I took 275, many of whom experienced great cures. Take Nan, for instance:

"I had migraines for 20 years, but after coming down from the King's Chamber, I haven't had a headache since."

Bill noted:

"For 37 years I've led a life of tortured depression. After visiting Cheops, I've never been depressed again."

And even more dramatically, Susan wrote:

"I had suffered with such painful arthritis that going up the Grand Gallery, I thought I'd just die . . . but on the descent, I didn't have any pain and haven't since."

Even deeper psychological changes have taken place on these trips, as some people viewed their past lives and even unloaded old grudges or pains of betrayal. There have also been at least seven breakups of marriage—including my own. I believe that the Sphinx and Egyptian pyramids mirror us favorably or unfavorably, reflecting ourselves back to us. All in all, I've taken about 700 people to Egypt, and at least two-thirds have come back changed and with a feeling of deeper spirituality (even if not everyone's experience was as dramatic as Nan's, Bill's, or Susan's).

I truly believe that somehow, as I mentioned earlier, there is implanted knowledge in those rocks—I mean, if all nature, including us, comes with a cell memory, why couldn't the stones carry information that we'll someday be able to tap in to?

I always smile when I see how smug some people are about our technology, especially when we haven't yet scraped the surface of ancient wisdom. We don't even know how to preserve bodies like the ancient Egyptians did. What's interesting is how many people living today have had a past life in Egypt. (The same is true for Lemuria and Atlantis.) Since Africa is the seat of the beginnings of most of our lives on Earth—or at least a life or two stopover, especially for those seeking knowledge of ancient spiritual beliefs— I guess this makes sense.

The three pyramids standing in a row on the plain of Giza— one large (father), one smaller (mother), and another even smaller (child)—are a trinity standing in the desert. While no jewels or treasure were found here, the edifices that stand show humankind something far more precious: that our trials and tribulations take us to our ascension. In fact, in 1954 at the base of the Great Pyramid, archaeologist Kamal el-Mallakh found what they now refer to as a "solar boat," which was intended to be used by the pharaohs to traverse the skies. How could they have known that something (or *someone* for that matter) could fly with a boatlike object unless they'd seen it?

The Sphinx

The next sacred site I explored was the Sphinx. It seems that every scientist in the world has had his or her opinion on whose face it represents. I don't believe that it was any one person's face. First of all, the Sphinx is the guardian of the temple (the Great Pyramid), and it symbolizes the eternity of humankind surviving and looking out over the desert of life; also, consider how many of the Egyptian gods were part human and part animal.

Here, I'm delivering a lecture at the base of the Sphinx.

I believe that this was to show how humans could "morph" into a type of totem, to take on the qualities of animal *and* human and combine the two from bravery to cunning or strength. This, of course, could then make a person more godlike—much like our Christian saints or even Christ himself being called the "lamb of God."

Francine dropped a bombshell when she told me that the Ark of the Covenant is buried beneath what's left of the Sphinx. (After all, what better place to hide the Ark than beneath the Sphinx, where no one would think to look for it?) Since the Ark was made of wood and gold, it conducted some kind of electrical current because it housed so many secrets about life and how it should be lived. It even contained plans on how the Sphinx and Egyptian pyramids were built—it was almost like a small reference library.

Even though I had no problem with the information I'd received on the Great Pyramid, I did have some concerns about the Ark being under the Sphinx. However, when I went back with my wonderful friend Abass Nadim (who, God love him, is now on the Other Side—and that's a story in itself) in 2001 and 2002, Dr. Zahi Hawass told Abass and me that some Egyptologists were beginning to look beneath the Sphinx and had found a hidden room, but there was some problem or diplomatic confusion that was holding up the excavation.

Abass said, "Sylvia, the fact that you knew there was a room beneath the Sphinx is remarkable, especially when no one heretofore believed that anything was there."

Someday I know they'll find the Ark here. Maybe the tablets are in it, but even if they aren't, I'm convinced that there's enough evidence to prove its authenticity—and this theory.

Other Pyramids and Tombs

About a thousand miles south of Cairo, in present-day Sudan, are the Nubian pyramids. There are twice as many pyramids in the Sudan as there are in Egypt (about 180). The Nubians even ruled Egypt at one time for about 60 years. Their pyramids were interestingly enough called the "resurrection machines" and were used as burial places for their kings and nobles.

There are indications that extraterrestrials had a hand in cultures throughout Egypt and Africa. (This also makes sense when you find a culture such as the Dogan tribe in Mali, which had no telescopes but knew extensively about Sirius, or the Dog Star, and its surrounding stars—and they claimed that their gods came from there, too. How would such a supposedly "primitive" tribe know about a faraway star unless someone came from the heavens to show them?)

Francine says that if you look at a map, you'll see that pyramids form a triangle from the jungles of the Yucatán in Mexico to Peru to Giza; they were also used as a sort of telegraph station. She said that in the beginning, all the pyramids had crystals on top (which have eroded over time), and that's how the ancient people communicated with each other.

I find it incredible that these cultures, which were separated by continents, would erect similar edifices. How could they know how to do this unless there was one intelligence that instructed them? In *Chariots of the Gods,* author Erich Van Daniken shows what he says appears to be a carving of a man wearing a space helmet at a control panel.

This carving was found on the stone lid of the sarcophagus of the great Mayan king Pacal, which can be found in the ruins of the ancient Mayan city of Palenque in present-day Mexico. His grave was found inside a pyramid-shaped temple and was the first tomb found in any Mayan pyramid. Archaeologists have begun to decipher the carving, which is said to represent Pacal's going to the afterlife. They think that a tree in the background of the carving symbolizes the Milky Way, with Pacal in all his glory going toward it in his heavenly vehicle.

Again, scientists are reluctant to admit that it is in fact a spaceship in this carving. Well, I ask you, what in ancient times could possess an ancient Mayan to depict someone with a bubble on his head sitting at what looks like a control panel in a heavenly vehicle with fire coming out from underneath? I could understand pictures of harvesting and picking corn, drawing oxen, and so forth, but not something as sophisticated as this. And once again, we see different cultures who supposedly had no knowledge of each other building with similar techniques and designs. There *had* to have been some messenger or outer-space culture that showed these primitive peoples how to build such complex edifices.

It's also interesting to note that several servants were buried with Pacal, just as servants were buried with the Nubians and Egyptians. Also, recent excavation of Incan mummies in Peru found them to be as preserved, if not more so, than Egyptian mummies, with afterlife the main reason for their mummification. Many of the mummies were found buried together or in close proximity. Without fishing too much, if Jim Jones could coerce more than 900 people to die with him in Guyana, why couldn't a leader get his people to not only build him a tomb because he was a "god," but to also die and be buried with him?

I never paid much attention to these glaring similarities until I began to research them; and when I did, I found my mouth dropping open more than once. (Even if you don't buy any of this, it makes wonderful reading and a great history lesson.) Consider the following:

— In China in 1974, a farmer digging a well found thousands of terra-cotta warriors buried in a huge underground vault. Chinese scientists determined that these warriors were guarding the grave of an ancient emperor who was inside the tomb. Inside, they found not only thousands of these beautifully handcrafted warriors, but also an elaborate monument with rivers of mercury and even "stars" made of pearls in the heavens above the burial chamber. They're afraid to excavate in earnest, fearing damage to the site and the beautiful tomb.

— In Egypt, there are many tombs not only in the Valley of the Kings, but also around Amarna, which was the Egyptian capital founded by Akhenaten and where his tomb is supposedly located. (Akhenaten, for those of you who don't know, was the pharaoh who introduced monotheism to the Egyptians.)

Although Akhenaten's tomb has been discovered, there's still no scientific evidence that his *body* has been recovered, for his tomb was partially incomplete—and even though some scientists believe that they found his body and the remains of his family, others are highly skeptical, for the body is of a young man. To date, most scientists still believe that Akhenaten hasn't been found. I mention these burial places because pyramids have always been associated with tombs—yet evidence is now coming to light that the pyramids weren't used just for burial.

— Another similarity that gives fuel to the fire of extraterrestrial influence is in the actual building of these huge edifices in different parts of the world. The Incan and Mayan building methods have great similarity, especially in the laying of stones that are so closely jointed that no mortar is necessary, and in the size of the stones that reach multiple tons in weight.

In the article "Egyptologists: It Is Time to Prove Your Claims" (published on **www.world-mysteries.com**), independent investigative journalist Will Hart claims that Egyptologists display irrational and unscientific fixations that the ancient Egyptian builders quarried, transported, lifted, dressed, and precisely positioned blocks of stone weighing 50 to 200 tons. He says the problem is that it hasn't been proven that the primitive tools and methods that the builders were believed to have used were equal to the task. In fact, several well-documented attempts over the past 30 years have failed to replicate what the early Egyptian builders achieved. We must also realize here that we certainly have the technology to build giant buildings and great bridges, yet we can't seem to duplicate a pyramid.

As Mr. Hart explains, in the 1970s, a Japanese team funded by Nissan tried to build a one-third scale model of the Great Pyramid using the methods that the Egyptologists claimed the ancient engineers employed. The Japanese team couldn't duplicate a single step of the process; in fact, they couldn't duplicate *any* steps without modern machinery, and even that failed miserably. The

failure showed that the simple tools and equipment that were supposedly used by early humans could not have built the pyramids.

The team came back in the 1990s to try to raise an obelisk,
again using the crude instruments and equipment that Egyptologists claim did the work. (The largest obelisk in Egypt weighs
approximately 400 tons, but the Japanese decided to raise one that
weighed 35 tons, a considerable difference in size and weight.)
First of all, they failed to carve their obelisk using the dolomite ham-
mers that scientists believe the Egyptians used—the Japanese team
carved theirs using a bulldozer; second, they couldn't use a boat for
transportation, so they used a large truck (you can see how this is
going); and finally, they tried to lift the obelisk in place and failed.

To be fair, this same team did come back several years later,
and by eliminating the first two steps of quarrying and transportation, they managed to get the obelisk up after two tries. Suffice
it to say, they proved a point: that these ancient monuments were
not built by the ancient Egyptians with their rudimentary tools.

Scientists, engineers, and Egyptologists have scratched their
heads in wonder when they come face-to-face with the problem
of just how these giant edifices were built. Many of the same are
now coming up with alternative theories on how the pyramids were
constructed, but again the vast majority still thinks that the
ancient Egyptians did the building with stone chisels and ham-
mers, ropes, thousands of slaves going up ramps, and so forth.

It seems that no one wants to be brave or honest enough to
say, "I just don't know" or "Maybe it could have been built by a
superior intelligence." After all, God was always supposed to
live in the sky, so could it be possible that the reason this theory
originated (other than the fact that He or She is always around
us) is because this Superior Intelligence descended from above?

Mr. Hart is nothing if not controversial, but he sticks to his guns and says that we have a hard time moving 300-ton pieces of stone today—even with all our technology—and that we "may as well believe [that the ancient Egyptians] used teleportation." He also implies that many Egyptologists today don't come clean about what they know or don't know, due to social, political, and scientific pressures.

It seems that those who have questioned popular theories have either been blackballed or called downright frauds. Such was the case with Michael Cremo, who put together a controversial documentary challenging the building of the Egyptian pyramids. When his film was aired, NBC was deluged with calls by scientists who called him a completely unscientific sham.

Dr. Virginia Steen-McIntyre was another maverick who offered controversial data that wasn't unlike that of Hart and Cremo. She was asked to retract her information, and when she refused, she lost her job at an American university. Scientists today are much like doctors—that is, their organizations hold a lot of power to suppress new information and truths, and God help them if they try to buck the system, even if they have the best intentions of science and impeccable credentials.

Nevertheless, *anyone* can be a researcher or even a scientist. You don't have to have initials after your name to come up with a process or theory—just record the facts until you get, as it were, more nays than yeas or vice versa. For example, in Will Hart's article, he issued a challenge to Egyptologists to prove their long-held theory of how the pyramids were built. He states:

> This brings up the issue of The Big Lie and how it has been promoted for generations in front of God and everyone. The

controversy over how the Great Pyramid was constructed is one example. It could be easily settled if Egyptologists wanted to resolve the dispute. A simple test could be designed and arranged by impartial engineers that would either prove or disprove their longstanding disputed theory—that it was built using the primitive tools and methods of the day, circa 2500 B.C.

Some have tried and failed to do just that, which leaves us with what I've observed and documented many times . . . no, I'm not a scientist, nor do I profess to be, but I *am* a researcher who believes without a doubt that the pyramids at Giza were built by beings from another galaxy with far more knowledge than we've ever possessed. Francine says that these beings are from Andromeda—that may very well be, but whether from there or another star system, I firmly believe that no one on this planet built these structures by themselves. In fact, I think that visitations from outer space were common to ancient and primitive man.

Aliens interacted with ancient humans because primitive people already believed that God came from the sky, so it wasn't unusual for them to accept extraterrestrial visits. However, after the advent of the One God, an alien might have appeared to Moses in a burning bush, but that was about the end of it . . . except for Elijah, who "went up to heaven" in a "chariot of fire." (2 Kings 2:11). Many scientists have tried to duplicate the way Elijah's journey was described in the Bible, and they came up with a machine that looked like a space vehicle, but they didn't know how to make it go.

I believe that these beings of higher intelligence brought us their spiritual knowledge, perhaps even that the soul lives on and goes into the heavens. (You must realize that the Egyptians aren't true reincarnationists—the reason they were called so is because they believed in life after death, which is why the tombs were filled with every part of the pharaoh's life so that he could come back and enjoy it. However, they didn't believe that life continued in a circle of rebirth as the Hindus, Buddhists, and Essenes—of which Christ was part—did.)

Francine says that extraterrestrials colonized us—and she told me this when I was about ten years old. I wasn't too interested then, but I thought it sounded as good as anything else I'd heard, so I filed it away. Later on, I was floored to discover that Edgar Cayce had said the same thing as Francine. Now, how does that affect the chart we wrote for ourselves before we came in? It doesn't: We just chart what planet to come into and what we have to learn while we're on it. (As an aside, Francine did say that anyone who comes to this planet is the bravest of the brave and learns faster than anywhere else because this is the insane asylum of the universe. The older I get, and the more I see and hear, the more I know in my soul that this is true. But take heart—it just means that those of us who chose to come here were not only courageous, but we also wanted to graduate faster. Spiritually, we can make a good case for all the messengers, such as Christ, Buddha, and Mohammed, who came here to preach love and peace. I don't want to be negative, but sometimes it seems that so many just haven't learned. . . .)

It's interesting to note that we received so much superb knowledge from ancient astronauts who came down from heaven; yet, as human beings became more civilized, we stopped accepting the sightings. However, we'll see aliens surface again in the next ten years or so. Yet since humankind will have a hard time accepting this, and because the way of the world is, they could be shot down as terrorists. Ultimately, in around 2050, our celestial friends will start to work among us.

I think it's time to close this chapter, although we could research these particular mysteries for years. But like I've always said: Take the facts and read and come to your own conclusions—you just may come to the same realizations that I have. Whatever you decide, know that the entire region that encompasses the pyramids—including the people and even the sand—seems to carry a mystical air. This was a place, like all of Africa, where life began, and it guards its secrets with almost an oxymoron of friendly hostility. It's as if they know that no matter what science tries to prove, their gods not only came from the skies, but showed them how to lay bricks without mortar that would last longer than any edifice the world has ever known.

A crop circle on the Salisbury plain near Stonehenge.

18
Crop Circles

For hundreds of years, the crop-circle phenomenon has surfaced periodically. A few years ago it made its way back in the news thanks to the movie *Signs* with Mel Gibson. To be honest with you, I used to vacillate back and forth on whether or not human beings were responsible for creating these intricate circles. Certainly many scientists have caught people making these shapes on camera, but keeping that in mind, let's look at some of the facts—and then you can make your own decision.

⋅⋅∞⋅⋅

First of all, crop circles have been around for a very long time and have been seen in many countries around the globe. Although they're mostly associated with the British Isles (since most of them have appeared there), crop circles have also been found in the United States, Africa, Europe, Australia, Central and South America, Japan, Canada, and Russia. Almost every continent has had them in one form or another, and they seem to be getting more sophisticated and complex in design.

One of the earliest and most well-known accounts of a crop circle is documented in a woodcut made in England in 1678, which was titled "The Mowing-Devil: Or Strange News Out of Hartford-shire." Long before the camera was ever invented, this rendering depicted a devil-like creature cutting out a pattern in a field with a scythe. The text on the woodcut tells the story of a greedy farmer who didn't want to pay the going rate to a local mower, so he allegedly said that he'd rather have the devil do the harvesting. The next morning, the farmer awoke to find that his crop had indeed been harvested—but in a strange manner, with circles that no human being could have done in one night.

The circles were so exact and in such perfect symmetry that the farmer and local townspeople were sure it was the work of the devil. The farmer was so afraid that he didn't even enter the field to gather his harvest. (Even though this story seems far-fetched, the woodcut does in fact exist, and the reaction of the principal characters is consistent with the time period; after all, anything that couldn't be explained was considered the work of the devil.)

Some cryptologists and other scientists hypothesize that many crop-circle patterns are also found in prehistoric stone and wall carvings. Examples of this are the spiral carvings in a stone at New-grange in Ireland (shades of Stonehenge, with something or someone coming from the heavens). Others point to ancient and

inexplicable pictures such as those made by the Nazca people in the Peruvian desert and suggest similarities to crop circles.

There is also proof that some of these configurations are depicted in some very ancient Egyptian pictures. I personally saw these on the walls of tombs and in the ancient temples in Karnak. I even mentioned to a few of the people I traveled with that those pictures looked like crop-circle configurations.

I know this all seems almost too circumstantial, but as we travel through these mysteries and go further back, we'll notice a common thread that binds all this information together. As the ancient Druids pointed to the heavens, so did the Egyptians and even the early Celts—thus, we see the pattern emerging: *We are not alone.*

I've really come to believe that crop circles are geometric and mathematical configurations from people from other planets. I also believe that some of them are maps to a galaxy or planet configuration that perhaps we're not aware of. Some of the patterns almost look like musical notes, and I believe that whoever is making them is trying to communicate with us.

I don't want to get too heavily into UFOs here, but even though they've caught people creating or trying to duplicate crop circles, there are too many to be discounted as hoaxes—and just like in the 1600s, it's totally impossible for any group of people to make these huge, precise patterns in one night.

Some Crop-Circle Theories

There are many theories behind the origin of crop circles—some seem to be logical, while others are so far out as to be ridiculous. One theory along these lines is the so-called Gaia hypothesis, which says that Mother Earth is mad at the way we're treating her, so the formations are her way of telling us that we've got to change our ways. Proponents of this theory insist that most of the circles are found near sacred sites, such as in Stonehenge, where the earth's energies are strongest. While I disagree with this theory, it's a fact that many of the crop circles *are* made near sacred sites around the world. I feel that whoever is making them chooses these locations to place more emphasis on what they're trying to do.

Another theory that has been put forth is the Plasma Vortex Theory, in which it is theorized by Dr. Terrance Meaden that the spiral patterns occurring in crop circles are due to atmospheric phenomena such as the vortex of a dust devil or tornado. Well, I come from Missouri and have seen many dust devils and tornadoes in my time, but I've never seen them make a crop circle. Common sense says that these types of violent storms suck up matter, leave devastation, and are always random in nature—they don't make perfect circles or other configurations, such as intricate pictures with straight lines, curves, and so forth.

Other theories that get good press but seem to be "out there" are military experimentation; underground archaeological digs; and, of course, the mainstay for skeptics—hoaxes. Let's examine them one by one.

1. **Military experimentation** is a good one, for everything that's unexplained is now theorized to be the work of some great secret military experiment. Use common sense again: Crop circles have been found all over the world in *many* countries—no one government's military experiment would be able to do that.

A conspiracy of several governments? Think again. We can't get along in everyday life, let alone enjoy military cooperation with foreign governments. Nix this theory—it isn't practical, nor is it worth our time to pursue it.

2. As far as the **underground archaeological** theory goes, crop circles are in too many places with different locales for this to be pertinent. It's also somewhat preposterous to believe that archaeological sites, fascinating as they may be, can cause the intricate designs of crop circles (which we'll touch on a little later).

3. This brings us to **hoaxes.** Now, top experts in crop-circle phenomena (such as Colin Andrews) all agree that *some* of the circles were made by human hands—but that doesn't mean *all* of them were. In fact, the evidence for crop circles being made by some nonhuman force or intelligence gets stronger all the time. Let me tell you why.

The hoax theory began in earnest in the early 1990s in England, when two buddies named Dave Chorley and Doug Brower confessed to making about 200 circles in various locations in the British Isles. The two contended that they made the configurations with board planks and rope, and they'd been making them for the last 13 years. The media ate this up; and as Dave and Doug became celebrities of a sort overnight, the press immediately took the stance that *all* crop circles were humanmade hoaxes. Additional pranksters came out of the woodwork and proceeded to make circles of their own. In the midst of this circus, genuine researchers were hard-pressed to back up their own theories and try to get crop circles back on a genuine scientific plane.

Let me stop here briefly to explain something very important. Do not, I repeat, *do not* believe all that you hear from television, newspapers, magazines, and the like. If you do, you'll often miss the truth. Being under constant media scrutiny myself, I know firsthand how many mistakes the press in general makes by jumping in quickly without proper investigation. I have many friends who are celebrities and many who are scientific researchers, and the horror stories they've related to me about misrepresentation, misreporting of facts, and downright lies are mind-boggling.

This entire journalism profession has one big problem that they try to push under the rug, but can't—and that's that they're in their business for profit. This results in stories being released quickly in order to "scoop" the competition, which then leads to falsehoods and poor research. It also culminates in stories being fabricated, pictures being falsified, quotes being misrepresented or made up, and a general unprincipled attitude.

It's unfortunate that the media has such power to influence people in so many ways without repercussions. Sure, retractions are put on the last page of the newspaper or at the end of a news broadcast—but by that time, the damage has already been done. Such was the case with crop circles and the hoax frenzy perpetuated by the media.

In the end, good old Dave and Doug recanted their confessions after threats of being sued by outraged farmers. It turns out that they only admitted to making about a dozen crop circles, but by then it was too late. Despite the recantation and the fact that more than 200 crop circles had been reported over the previous 13 years (and many before that time), the media gave this part of the story little coverage. In the meantime, there were now many "hoaxers" out there doing their thing. The problem was that they couldn't duplicate true crop circles.

You see, when the whole phenomenon of the circles started, they were fairly simplistic in nature. This continued for several decades; then, inexplicably, the patterns began to become more complex. This change in the complexity of crop circles more or less coincided with the hoax frenzy coming to light. It was almost as if those who really made them were determined to prove that they weren't created by human beings. Many think that the actual creatures are trying to communicate with us. The following should help you understand why I think crop circles are made by an intelligent extraterrestrial entity, and it should help convince the skeptics out there.

— Crop circles have been discovered mostly in barley and wheat crops, but they've also appeared in corn, oats, canola, grass, rice fields, trees, sand, and even snow. They've been found in more than 70 countries around the globe—many near ancient or sacred sites. Inexplicably, many farmers have reported greater yields (a 30 to 40 percent increase) in their crops in the years following the appearance of formations in their fields.

— Freddy Silva, an author, researcher, and lecturer, has written an article called "So It's All Done with Planks and Bits of String, Is It?" explaining many crop-circle basics. He maintains that there have been nearly 10,000 documented crop circles across the globe, although about 90 percent of them appeared in southern England. Of course, many have not been reported. He theorizes that these circles are now "mimicking computer fractals and elements that relate to fourth-dimensional processes in quantum physics." He also says that the sizes of crop circles have increased with their complexity in the past ten years or so, and some have been as large as 200,000 square feet.

Silva says that in general, circles found in the British Isles are formed between the hours of 2 and 4 A.M.—especially during the times of year when the evenings are short and darkness only lasts about four hours. He also tells of a strange occurrence for which there is photographic evidence:

> At Stonehenge in 1996, a pilot reported seeing nothing unusual while flying above the monument, yet 15 minutes later this huge 900 ft. formation resembling the Julia Set computer fractal, and comprising 149 meticulously layed *[sic]* circles, lay beside the well-patrolled monument. It took a team of 11 researchers including myself nearly five hours just to *survey* the formation.

In his article, Silva also claims that researchers at NASA have confirmed an artificial "trilling" sound recorded at crop-circle sites, which corresponds to the fact that some eyewitnesses claim to have heard such a noise coming from the direction of the formations.

— Crop circles have appeared in restricted areas that are heavily patrolled. Military installations that are fenced and patrolled have had formations, as has a field in the country estate of the British Prime Minister in 1991, which was guarded by special antiterrorist troops.

— Numerous eyewitnesses to crop-circle formations have reported that sounds and light accompany the process, and some have even witnessed circles being made in as little as 20 seconds! Some have also described large balls of brilliant color that project a beam of golden light into a field that reveals a new crop circle.

When I was in England, many people told me that they were convinced that crop circles are from out of this world. One family that I heard from—who were just plain, good, hardworking farmers—got up in the morning to find the most intricate formations that you could ever imagine. The symmetry was impeccable, the measurements in every area were perfect in every radius, and so on. I don't see how a human (or humans) with ropes and boards could make such a wonderful formation . . . which, of course, they can't. Even though teams of volunteers have tried to duplicate these formations, they just can't—it's as simple as that.

The people I've talked to said that when they visited the circles, they became dizzy. Some experienced euphoria, some nausea, but everyone felt *something*. Not all of these people (including respected scientists) could feel these effects and still be accused of having dramatic flights of fancy. And skeptics can't explain why we can't find footprints leading into or out of the fields; why all the stalks of the plants are bent in perfect order, yet undamaged; or why highly complex layers of interwoven stalks are often found in a perfectly symmetrical design.

Finally, no one seems to want to mention that when people use Geiger counters, they go off the chart. The residual energy at these sites has an almost radioactive effect, like a microwave. Since researchers have found that this energy is affecting crops by increasing yields, this shows me that whether the soil is purified or radiated, it does nothing but help the land. (Now, how would people from this planet leave behind radiation?)

———✦———

I remember once when I was on a shoot at a haunting and Terry, our cameraman, had just come back from filming crop circles. He and his crew had just found two round discs in the soil of the circles, and this information was reported in the newspaper (albeit in a small paragraph). Terry later told me that two men came to his door, flashed a badge, and confiscated the discs. He told me that he wished he'd questioned it more, but he was afraid.

I don't mean to imply that there's a conspiracy, but I do feel that our government thinks we're stupid—or maybe they believe that information about these formations will cause panic. What I don't understand is if someone wants to converse with us, why don't we try to help them or investigate the situation instead of just sweeping it under the carpet?

Consider again why crop circles show up around sacred sites like the sand near the pyramids or in the fields next to Stonehenge. Extraterrestrials are using these sites to try to get their message across. Computer and mathematical geniuses are attempting to decipher the configurations as we speak, and the designs seem to be some type of, for lack of a better word, hieroglyphs or picture words. Francine says that not only are they trying to communicate by symbols, but they're also trying to show where they're from in the galaxy. It reminds me of trying to understand the Rosetta stone.

Someday, when science gets with it, we'll see that these other-wordly beings are sending us love, but Francine says that with the tremendous violent outbreaks on Earth recently, they're also trying to show us that they're watching us and warning us of the danger of mistreating our planet.

Instead of trying to discredit crop circles, why don't we try to find out the common thread or scientific principle that binds them all together? I know it's being worked on, and I feel that in the next two years, not only will we see more of the circles worldwide, in more intricate patterns, but we'll also get more signs that we're not alone . . . and never have been.

Another formation from a different part of the world.

Part IV

Mystic Phenomena

19

Spontaneous
Human
Combustion

This bizarre phenomenon occurs when, for no reason whatsoever, a human body suddenly bursts into flames. Scientists can't understand how someone who's just sitting or standing there—not smoking or near any type of fire—can all of a sudden combust, causing their entire body to turn into cinders.

The body actually cremates itself, so in order for this to happen, the temperature would have to be in the thousands of degrees; yet, astonishingly, none of the surrounding area is burned or even singed in many cases. You'd think that with this much heat, everything around the victim would be charred—not so. Candles have even been found to be sitting on a mantel near a victim, unmelted. And amazingly enough, the victim's feet, hands, or fingers are often left untouched.

Reported cases have come out of Germany, America, the British Isles, and Australia, yet there's no pattern explaining why it happens—atmospheric conditions, specific locations, topography, and even types of fabric haven't provided a single clue. Spontaneous Human Combustion (called "SHC" in parapsychology) has been called the devil's work; as if there is a devil (which, as I've mentioned, there isn't) who doesn't have anything better to do than combust someone.

Of course, upon hearing about this phenomenon, I went straight to Francine for answers. She said that SHC is caused by a buildup of phosphorous, which is highly flammable—that's what causes the body to implode upon itself and start burning from the inside out.

I've talked to scientists who allow that the human body is made up of so many minerals and elements that if too much iron is present, for example, we'll die; or if we have too much copper, our liver will fail. So why couldn't we have too much phosphorous (which, by the way, is used in fireworks due to its high combustibility) and just implode?

It's interesting to note that phosphorous burns with high heat and intensity, as do most metals, such as sodium (just expose some to the air and see what happens) and magnesium. This would explain why, if the body did start to incinerate inside, the power of the fire would literally burn up the body, but not necessarily any of the surrounding area, as the intensity would immediately cease once the phosphorous in the body was gone.

Now, I don't think that we all need to go out and get tested for our phosphorous content—we have about as much chance of spontaneously combusting as we do of riding a unicorn with Mel Gibson over a rainbow (although that's not a bad visual!).

20
Kinetic Energy and Auras

Kinetic energy is used by people to move objects, sometimes by will or just at random, without them even being aware that they're doing so. I've talked to many clients who have this skill—they can make lightbulbs pop, computers crash, and objects move; and many can't even wear watches.

The Russians worked on kinetic energy quite a bit during their research on parapsychology, studying individuals who could make objects move with concentration. And years ago in the old Spiritualist camps, people who could harness kinetic energy were known as *physical mediums*. They'd be locked in a cabinet and monitored, and then things would begin to move. The problem was that physical mediums' power was random and sometimes couldn't be controlled that well; unlike the spiritual medium, who uses clairvoyance, clairaudience, and the ability to see the spirit world—and who seems to have much more control.

Many times, physical mediums were reported to exude *ectoplasm* (a white, sticky substance) when encountering a ghost. I'm not a physical medium, but the late Marcel Vogel, a scientist from IBM, once told me that when my energy gets too high, I burn film. I've also been known to bust klieg lights (special lights used in filming) in studios. When I used to do the show *People Are Talking* in San Francisco, it seemed that at least every other time I was on, I'd blow a light. I learned to tone down the energy once I was aware that I was doing this.

Anyway, once I was on a haunting investigation at the Brookdale Lodge near Santa Cruz, California, when, in front of three witnesses, I was slimed by ectoplasm. I wasn't eating, drinking, or carrying anything that could have made this substance appear all over the front of my blouse, and it happened when I was talking to a very cranky spirit I'd contacted who called himself "Judge" (and who was later historically validated as a real person who had resided in the lodge).

I kept talking to Judge, and even though I felt a film come over me, I didn't realize what had happened until I turned around and Michael (my secretary), my husband at the time, and a lodge employee exclaimed almost in unison, "Look at the front of your suit!"

Why do ghosts exude this substance? It's because their atmosphere sometimes becomes so condensed that it seems to form a "think" substance—almost as if their anger takes a form (much like the phrase "He was spitting mad").

Physical mediums have it very hard, because kinetic energy is so random. One celebrated psychic of the last century was noted to be a most authentic physical medium, but during one session when nothing happened (as it had so many times before), she resorted to kicking a chair over, and ruined a career that had spanned many years.

Then there's Uri Geller, a physical medium who, regardless of what anyone believes, I know is for real—I've worked with him and have seen what he does. Unfortunately, he came along before his time, and the skeptics have had a field day with him.

The mediums who *can* harness kinetic energy are far better off channeling it into healing, because they carry such an electrical charge that they can replace someone's energy and create a cure.

Nevertheless, even with the few experiences I've had that shows me it's real, I'm so thankful to God that I'm a spiritual medium and don't have to wait for kinetic energy to come and create a physical phenomenon.

Auras

Auras are really nothing more than the electrical emanations that surround us. I've never really bought into the idea of Kirlian photography that can supposedly photograph auras, as it's too inconsistent and really doesn't indicate much (although someday we will have aura scanners to diagnose illness).

It's funny how we speak in terms of auras: "I feel blue today," "That person has a sparkling personality," "I was so mad, I saw red!" And so many times we use color or aura language to express ourselves: a "gray" day, a "golden" time, and so on. Yet we really do emit colors in our auras: Red means we're angry; green indicates that we're healing, either ourselves or others; blue points to serenity; and purple means that we're communing with God or are spiritual. But auras can change with our moods day by day (or hour by hour).

People who are always seeing auras worry me because that could indicate that they have an eye disease. To see an aura once in a while is more normal than you might realize, but most of the time, it's more authentic to *feel* it: We tune in to someone's darkness or lightness. If we listen to our inner feelings, we'll be just as accurate as if we try to see the emanation of an aura around everyone.

21

Voodoo, Astrology, and Shamans

Although it might seem strange that I've lumped these three topics in one chapter, they have all been horribly vilified and misunderstood over the years, yet they're actually quite positive.

Voodoo

We certainly can't get into all the spiritual practices of every religion, as that would be a book in itself, but voodoo has always been a mystery to the Western world.

Two of the best documentations of the practice are probably *Drum and Candle* by David St. Clair and *The Serpent and the Rainbow* by Wade Davis (which was also made into a movie directed by Wes Craven). Other than these books, we know very little about the practice of voodoo. And although both of the aforementioned works have great merit, they also have some erroneous drama thrown in, such as zombies, curses, and so on. In fact, most of what's been written about voodoo has been wrong.

Years ago, when I was getting my master's degree in English literature, I had a professor by the name of Bob Williams, who taught night school at the College of Notre Dame in Belmont, California. (We were very close and loved each other very much, but above all, he encouraged me to start a foundation. He died many years ago, and I miss him every day. I've always mourned his death because he was a brilliant, spiritual man who believed in me and my powers and encouraged me to go more public, rather than just reading for women's clubs and my family and friends.)

One night after class, Bob said that he'd heard about a voodoo meeting in San Francisco with a high priestess named Devlin. *What a name,* I thought, but after surrounding Bob and myself with the white light of the Holy Spirit, I decided to attend.

When we arrived at this apartment, the entire place was full of flower children. (This was in the days of the hippie movement in San Francisco, right before drugs took over.) Here I was in my schoolteacher dress, while Bob wore slacks and a shirt . . . I couldn't figure out if we were overdressed or underdressed. John Paul, a kind-looking young man with a beard, welcomed us and invited us to join everyone in a circle. A large cup of herbal tea was passed around, from which we all drank—it was like a communion of love. Then we meditated as we waited for the guest of honor to arrive.

Devlin was a high priestess of *voodone,* the proper name for voodoo. She was about 5'4", plump, with jet-black hair and very white skin, and she wore a black dress with a raven-wing belt. I looked at Bob as if to say, "Now what?!"

The priestess took a chair in the middle of the room and proceeded to pull on her left ear and let out the most awful snorting sound, which she claimed cleared her sinuses. *God help us,* I thought. Bob, sensing my anxiety (and knowing what might come out of my mouth), nudged me in the ribs. I'm not critical—except when people who are supposed to be teachers feel they have to be bizarre.

Devlin began to explain that voodoo was a religious practice that was very old and had existed in Africa for longer than recorded history. Followers believe that everything in nature carries energy (somewhat like the Wiccan belief), and the religion deals with spirits of the dead.

She went on to tell us that voodoo isn't just about casting spells of evil—on the contrary, it's steeped in Christianity, especially Catholicism. In fact, it's not unusual to see a statue of Jesus and the Blessed Virgin, as well as an altar to some spirit deity, as the high priest or priestess performs a ceremony. The spirits who possess a person, of which Devlin said there are many, ride the head of the recipient—which to me defies true possession. Such entities seem to just ride the head so that the host simply takes on the personality of the spirit.

I interrupted Devlin to ask her about bad spells; she hedged, but did say something I'll never forget—that belief is a powerful thing, and if people feel as if they've been cursed, then they begin to almost fulfill their own prophecy. She wouldn't comment on zombies except to say that she'd seen some and they were like individuals who had undergone a lobotomy.

Devlin continued with her talk, saying that the Pentacle of Solomon was used for protection, as was the sacrifice of the cutting off of a chicken's head and letting the blood drip in a circle (which does recall biblical sacrifice to God, something that was done often in the Old Testament). The entire voodoo religion was actually based on protection and asking God or spirit gods for what the people wanted.

I feel that the hysteria and "drums that go into the night" give rise to voodoo practitioners' bizarre performances, but in my studies, I've found that this religion has gotten a bad rap for curses (such as making people sick, and so on). Practitioners of voodoo *do* believe in curses and will do elaborate ceremonies to release them, but is this any different than exorcisms practiced by Catholics?

Voodoo is practiced extensively in Brazil, Haiti, and a lot of South American countries. One of their primary aims is to get rid of the devil (or evil) and align oneself with God or spirit gods for protection. Of course in modern-day medicine, we can treat the hearing of voices in the mentally unstable (oftentimes a symptom of schizophrenia) with medication and therapy, yet a person who was diagnosed with this illness might also be cured by a high priestess of voodoo.

The mind is a powerful, suggestive instrument that not only carries this life's negativity but past-life trauma as well. Who's to say that if life is like a phonograph record, and the needle slips into another groove, that a past-life regression or an exorcism might not remove an old behavior?

Devlin ended her talk, and we all kissed and left. The next week, the group of us waited and waited for Devlin, but she never showed up. Bob said, "Well, let's not disappoint them," so he announced that I'd do short readings for everyone. I decided that when we got outside, I'd either torture him or find ways to make his life miserable. Anyway, I must have done 30 quick readings, and everyone was happy.

As I was leaving, John Paul (who was almost like a holy man or angel) hugged me and said the words that still resonate with me: "Sylvia, your gift comes from God. Many people won't understand, and there are many ways to be crucified."

This was in the '60s—I had no way of understanding the ridicule, criticism, and scorn I'd go through. I still do at times, but I'm tougher now, so I pretty much let it roll off me; however, I've been such a target because of my gift and beliefs for so long now. As psychic medium John Edward once told me, "Sylvia, you tilled the field for all of us to come after you." I wanted to tell him, "You have no idea," but as the old saying goes, "What doesn't kill me just makes me stronger." What I do myself may seem mysterious to some, but I've always been me, so I just trust in God and go forward.

(As a side note, Devlin showed up on the third visit, but the participants wanted me to do more readings. So rather than causing friction and a jealous rage by the priestess, Bob and I excused ourselves and never went back.)

In conclusion, let me say that the religion of voodoo is greatly misunderstood. It's practiced in conjunction with Catholicism by most and is very spirit oriented, and it's also practiced by many who are very superstitious—which, of course, adds to its appeal and belief for some practitioners. Like all faiths, voodoo has its beautiful and wonderful side, as well as its dark aspects, which are grossly overexaggerated.

Astrology

To some people, astrology is a mysterious form of prophecy, and chronicling it is almost impossible. Long before recorded history, humankind looked to the heavens' enigmatic mix of galaxies, stars, and planets for answers. Somewhere along the way, ancient people began to correlate where the stars and the planets were positioned at the time of a baby's birth, which became known as the *natal chart.*

The Asian people seem to have been one of the first to have made astrology a type of science. They would go to their astrologer at almost the very minute their baby was born to see what was in store for the child, how to direct him or her, and even what he or she should avoid in life.

With the spread of Christianity, astrology had to go underground—only to resurface in the tea rooms (and back rooms) of the Western world. (Not so in China and Japan, where it flourishes to this day and apparently doesn't butt up against any religious belief.)

From the mathematical configurations of the natal chart, astrologers began to formulate what planets appeared at the time of birth, dividing them into 12 houses to determine not only an individual's personality, but also progressing the chart year by year to see where the planets would come into play and how they would affect that person's life.

The different birth configurations in the sky then began to take on the component parts of what the stars represented. For instance, if born under the sign of Taurus, a person was said to be stubborn like a bull; a Libra was seen to be balanced like the scales of justice; Virgo was pure like a virgin; Sagittarius was as fearless and outgoing as an archer; Leo was as proud and regal as a lion; Capricorn was as steadfast and steady as a goat; Aquarius was fluidly moving and artistic; Cancer was as tenacious and home-loving as a crab; Gemini had a dual nature, like twins; Aries was as fiery and headstrong as a ram; Scorpio was as intense as a scorpion—with as deadly a sting; and Pisces was as deep, psychic, and submerged in self as a fish.

I myself wrote an astrology book with a lot of truth in it *(Astrology Through a Psychic's Eyes)*, but it was also very tongue-in-cheek. I got more flack for saying that people born under the sign of Taurus could be boring—it was a joke, but many Taureans took offense . . . and they began to bore me with how wrong I was. (For God's sake, you Taureans, I'm a Libra, and we're ruled by the same planet—Venus!)

I like true astrology when it gets more specific: I don't place much stock in just telling trends, for that's not individualized. Yet the true astrologers whom I've met have convinced me that it also enhances their psychic ability and is a vehicle to open their sixth sense even further.

Shamans

A shaman is usually affiliated with the American Indian wise man (but very rarely a wise *woman*). This is the person, not unlike a modern-day priest, who listens to the transgressions of members of the tribe and offers advice. In the past, shamans were also known to make potions to heal and to get rid of evil spirits that they believed caused illness—by using rattles, smoke, feathers, seeds, or even snakeskins. They also could tell the future, both for individuals and for the entire tribe.

Now, there is some truth to the saying that if a person believes, that's half the cure, but I've seen some remarkable healings in Africa done by witch doctors (who are akin to the American Indian shaman). In fact, when some of the expatriates in Africa get sick, they're more often apt to call on a witch doctor than a traditional M.D. Sadly, these types of wise elders seem to be slipping into extinction, but they do have their place in certain tribes and seem to be very important to the well-being of their community. They also have the ability to go into trance (whether by their own means or via the use of some hallucinogen) and seem to be able to travel into the future and return with advanced knowledge.

Personally, I don't believe that we have to use any type of substance to see the future—but who am I to know or understand what works for shamans? I do know that they never used drugs for the purpose of recreation; instead, they were to be used sparingly in sacred ceremonies, and for greater knowledge. This is what LSD was originally designed for . . . then people began to use it for fun and "ate their brains out." Nevertheless, we should respect what the ancients knew and did and not try to copy something that we're ignorant of both physically and mentally— as well as spiritually.

22
Universal Enigmas

Let's take a moment here to explore a few of the mysteries that have confounded scientists as they've studied our ever-fascinating universe—including our beloved planet.

Black Holes

From the very first time they were discovered, black holes have piqued scientists' curiosity. Now, the great physicist Stephen Hawking has written extensively on this anomaly, but I like Francine's simplistic explanation, which she once gave to a group that was exploring certain mysteries of the universe. (I'm definitely a researcher, not a physicist, but I do get that the Other Side goes at a faster speed or a higher vibration than we do and that we're the world of transition and antimatter. However, I never quite understood the black-hole concept until Francine explained it.)

She said that first and foremost, a black hole is like the universe's vacuum cleaner: A star explodes (or implodes) and creates a type of crater in the atmosphere, piercing the veil of the universe and bringing everything around it into a funnel-like aperture, which then shows up in a parallel universe. In other words, there are universes backed up to this one, which is possibly the reason why we discover new stars or planets.

Next, the group asked Francine how all this fits into God's scheme, and she replied that there are planets all over the universe that are pushed through black holes to support life so that people can visit or reincarnate. With some holes, it's also a way of disposing of old planets that have turned into debris—so it's both a way of creating new life and getting rid of old useless junk, which to me is like a house cleaning or moving to another residence. God always keeps order in this vast home we call our universe.

Francine said that there are 44 universes; I don't think that matters to us, it's just for information. (It can make your head hurt to think of an infinity of universes linked together.) Francine says that we never leave our own cosmos, but we can visit others after we go to the Other Side. Many are different in configuration—some of the planets contain life while others don't (just like our own universe)—but regardless, God oversees it all.

The great thing about going to the Other Side is that we never quit researching and finding out new things about the magnitude of God's creation. That's also why the big bang theory is so wrong: Like us, the universe has always existed—maybe portions of it weren't initially ready for life (such as Earth), but it *was* always here. Scientists without a spiritual base (which isn't

their fault, it's their training) had to come up with some plausible explanation like the big bang theory, but why is it so hard to believe that if God always was, so was all of what God made? Otherwise, God is imperfect—and that's both untrue and illogical.

All this does give pause, at least to me, that when I do go Home, I can explore what are mysteries to us now, but open to us on the Other Side. It can make us feel small . . . until we remember that we are never small in God's eyes because He knows each one of us by soul progress, name, and chart.

The Polar Tilt

Approximately every 15,000 years or so, Earth goes into what I call a *polar tilt,* in which the axis of the planet shifts to a point at which the magnetic polarities change and move. At this time, great upheaval in the world's oceans and land masses can and do occur. The last polar tilt was in the time of the destruction of Atlantis and was also the cause of the "great flood" described in the Bible and other religious and historical texts.

A polar tilt also affects the planet's animal population as well as its weather. For example, as geologists know, the Sahara was once a very abundant part of Earth, yet today it's one of the driest places we know. And creatures that have followed migratory paths for hundreds of years are becoming confused; we now see, for instance, that the swallows are intermittently failing to come back to Mission San Juan Capistrano, in Southern California, where they used to show up every March 19 without fail.

We're also going to see more and more sea life beached—just like all those whales in California that, for no apparent reason, seemed to lose their way and died not long ago, regardless of how many marine biologists tried to save them. Even when they got some of the whales out to sea with the help of volunteers, the creatures turned around and beached themselves again. Did they want to die together, or were they convinced that they were going in the right direction because somehow their perception of topography had changed?

The polar tilt is also the reason for our strange climate changes. Right now, some areas of the world are enjoying very mild weather, while others endure harsh conditions—almost the opposite of what they normally get for different periods of the year. Aside from the greenhouse effect, people will be most affected by weather changes and more intensive natural disasters such as earthquakes, volcanic eruptions, and the rise and fall of land masses. Californians will be greatly affected, with massive land upheavals in about 20 or 30 years (although the polar tilt itself will take longer), and land will rise in the Atlantic. Although loss of life and extensive damage will be enormous, as always, humankind will survive.

The Hollow-Earth Theory

For many years, books such as *Journey to the Center of the Earth* by Jules Verne entertained the theory that not only is the earth hollow, but it also supports an entire civilization beneath its surface. Proponents of this theory are certainly in the minority as far as mainstream geologic thinking is concerned—most scientists say that our planet has a solid iron center surrounded by molten metal; and not to burst anyone's bubble, but I tend

to agree with that premise. From all the research I've done (through reading, hypnosis regressions, and Francine), I've never come across anyone who has lived in the middle of our planet.

Those who have put forth theories about a hollow earth have been labeled as crackpots, zealous "conspiracy plot" people, UFO nuts, and other descriptive terms in the same genre. I don't know if I'd go that far, as I've always been somewhat controversial in my own right and have put out some theories and information from my own research that certainly buck convention. I always try to keep an open mind in my skepticism, but I've yet to be convinced that this theory is correct.

ENLARGED

A UFO.

23
Alien Abductions

I'm not sure how I feel about alien abductions. I have a hard time believing that visitors to our planet would want to hurt us—if they can get here, they could certainly have done a lot of damage, yet they haven't. But since there have been too many reports of abductions to number, and I've lived long enough to never discount anything, I can't help but believe that some people have indeed been taken on board an alien ship.

Why are some people picked over others? I guess I could say the same for me—why should a girl from Kansas City be a psychic; or why, for that matter, is there a Pavarotti or a Picasso? Some individuals, I believe, are simply more likely receptors than others.

For example, Betty and Barney Hill were among the first abductees to gain notoriety in the press, and a TV movie was even made about their experiences. They didn't remember anything except losing time until they were hypnotized, and then they recounted in vivid detail about the experiments performed on them by the aliens who'd abducted them.

Nowadays, we hear about alien implants, alien babies, alien sexual practices, and alien you-name-it from Roswell to Arkansas. Most of these acts seem to occur in rural areas, and the reports seem to say pretty much the same thing: There were bright lights and lost time, then later the person starts showing depression, anxiety, terrible dreams, and partial amnesia. The use of hypnosis seems to ease the stress of the strange happenings.

I've spoken with many pilots, some of whom are retired, who haven't been allowed to talk about what they've seen because they were told that their retirement benefits will be taken away if they do. I don't necessarily think that all this is so much a government conspiracy (although they do know more than they're telling us) as much as it is their fear of putting out information that could throw the country—or the world—into a panic.

Personally, I think that the United States government underestimates our intelligence, and I used to wish that UFOs would just land in full view on the White House lawn—but then who's to say that someone wouldn't try to shoot them out of fear, a wish to protect themselves, or ignorance? Come to think of it, I guess the aliens have the right idea by not trusting the world to welcome them with open arms instead of weapons, especially in this day and age.

In 1938, when Orson Welles broadcasted "War of the Worlds," his famous radio show on the invasion from Mars,

there was a nationwide panic, and I really don't see that we're too far from that kind of hysteria today. Humans have always been afraid of the unknown, and the government doesn't want to advertise what they know because they fear that chaos will ensue.

In any case, one thing you can believe is what I've repeatedly said in this book: *We are definitely not alone in this universe—we never have been, and we never will be.*

22nd July, 1983 - Andover, UK. Colin Andrews

A UFO illuminated by lightning.

Part V

Christian Controversies

24
Stigmata

This mystery has existed for close to 2,000 years, seeming to arise after the Crucifixion of Jesus.

Stigmata is a condition in which the wrists or palms and feet (and in some instances, the side of the body) begin to exhibit gashes and/or bleeding in areas that are related to the wounds that Jesus received on the cross.

Although many laypeople have suffered stigmata, they all seem to be devout Catholics; it doesn't seem to be apparent in, or reported by, non-Catholics. In fact, we don't even tend to find it discussed anywhere except for Christian writings about individuals who apparently showed these injures in empathy with what Jesus suffered on the cross; for example, St. Francis of Assisi and the great healer and priest Padre Pio were said to have this "blessed affliction" (the Catholic phrase given to those who suffer stigmata).

At times, this phenomenon has been accompanied by an altered state of consciousness that's been called a state of "rapture" or form of trance. Stigmata has also been compared to those who practice injuring their bodies (such as self-flagellation) as a rejection of the physical shell they inhabit. In addition, stigmata is thought to be a manifestation of such love for Christ that people want to emulate his suffering—and it seems that many will do so on Friday, the day that Jesus was supposed to have died.

Stigmata can be termed a "miracle," or it can be a type of deep conviction or state of devotion that brings about a type of self-hypnosis. It's a known fact, as simplistic as it may sound, that you can hypnotize someone and tell them that you're putting a hot poker on their arm but instead apply an ice cube, and a high, angry blister will appear.

Now this isn't to say that miracles don't happen—God knows I've seen hundreds in my 50 years of practice—but I personally feel that individuals with stigmata are so imbued with their love of Jesus that they offer themselves to share his suffering. Those who exhibit these signs all seem to be more spirit than flesh, and no one who's ever had the wounds has been of ill repute; yet you find others who are very saintly (like Mother Teresa) who didn't have them at all. So it seems to be a level of inner devotion.

As I've said before, thoughts are truly things, and in all ways we become what we practice, feel, and think.

25
The Shroud of Turin

When I attended St. James grade school, I vividly recall an assembly in which two priests excitedly gave a presentation about the prospect that someone had found the linen sheet that covered Jesus at the time of his death. My fellow students and I were all mesmerized, for the Shroud of Turin was believed to be absolute proof positive to many Catholics (which I was at the time) that Christ had lived and died as the Gospels reported.

I went home and began to regale my grandmother with what I'd heard and seen. She looked up to the left for a minute, something I now do myself when I'm getting a

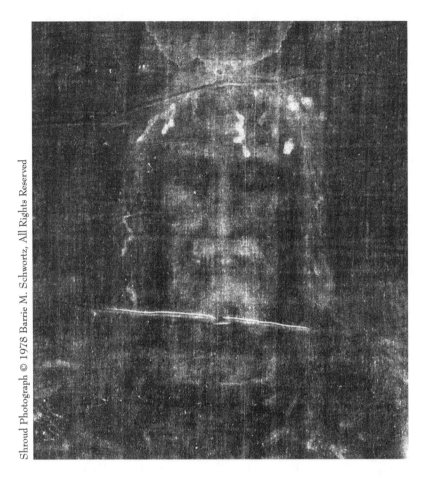

psychic feeling. (As an aside, a psychologist friend of mine, Dr. William Yarbroff, said after watching me do readings that I look to the left of the person when I pick up past events, look straight up when talking about the present, and look right when I'm reading the future—almost as if I'm searching for knowledge.)

In any case, Grandma Ada looked to the left and said, "Well, it's not Jesus. For one thing, the height is all wrong on the Shroud.

Also, he wasn't the only one crucified back then—countless people received that punishment." I knew my grandmother was picking this up psychically, as she had no prior information on the Shroud. I was somewhat disappointed, but I knew her and her track record well enough to believe that she was probably right.

The Shroud of Turin seemed to drop out of the cultural consciousness for a few decades—except when a die-hard few wanted to keep the mystique alive—then it made another resurgence into the public eye. The Shroud has gotten more press and scrutiny than any other Christian artifact, so it begs the question: "Do some not believe that there was a Christ; or, if there was, can we have proof positive that he did exist and die?" I personally don't think that Christianity needs a piece of cloth to confirm that a man by the name of Jesus Christ walked the earth, teaching love and peace.

There are actually two images on the Shroud, showing a man's back and front, which are separated by about eight inches of linen that doesn't exhibit any impression whatsoever. Skeptics point out that if these images were in fact made by energy from a body, why is there nothing shown in this gap?

It's noteworthy that some historians or theologians estimate that Jesus was around 5'6", which was the average height in Palestine at that time; however, the Shroud depicts a man who's about 5'11". It's also interesting to note that the Gospel of John says that when Christ was executed and supposedly died, the burial clothes were still in the tomb . . . but Jesus wasn't.

Some scientists believe that the Shroud was actually painted in the 14th century. After all, it was first known to exist in the year 1357, when it was in the possession of Geoffrey de Charny, a French knight who displayed it in a private chapel in Lirey in northeastern France. Some say that this knight was the heir of another Geoffrey de Charny, who was one of the Knights Templar and who had been executed by the Catholic Church for heresy and had all his possessions seized.

Suffice it to say, the younger Geoffrey was a man of modest means and never said where the Shroud came from. Because of this reluctance to talk about its origin, Bishop Pierre D'Arcis wrote a letter to Pope Clement VII saying that he thought the Shroud was a product of human handicraft—a cloth cunningly painted by a man. In 1389, Pope Clement VII decided that the cloth should be considered a "representation," not necessarily a true artifact.

If the Shroud were in fact painted, it would explain some image flaws that have always raised questions. For example, the hair hangs as for a standing rather than a reclining figure; the physique is unnaturally elongated (like figures in Gothic art); and the "blood" flows are unrealistically neat (instead of matting the hair, for instance, they run in rivulets on the outside of the locks). You see, real blood soaks into cloth and spreads in all directions rather than leaving picturelike images.

On top of all this, an examination of the "blood" in 1973 was done as part of a special commission of scientists and scholars, including the distinguished microanalyst Walter McCrone. Dr. McCrone found that there was no evidence of blood, but there *was* evidence of paint, so he quickly announced that the Shroud was a fake. But the problem didn't stop there, for Dr. McCrone's

findings were disputed by other scientists who said that the image did, in fact, contain blood—they even classified its type (AB). Further studies have most of the scientific community siding with those who believe that the blood in the images is real; most now refute the paint theory.

Then in January 1996, a discovery by Leoncio A. Garza-Valdes, M.D., and Stephen J. Mattingly, Ph.D., spurred new debate about the Shroud. The doctors discovered a layer of bacteria and fungi in almost a plastic-type coating on fibers from samples that they said were provided for the 1988 tests. They contended that these contaminants made carbon dating highly suspect and that the Shroud of Turin is much older than the tests indicated. (Carbon dating of the cloth was performed by three different laboratories, and they dated the Shroud as having been created anywhere from the years 1260 to 1390.)

This latest breakthrough has raised a new storm about the true age of the Shroud—skeptics say that it makes little if any difference, while proponents say that the preponderance of evidence now indicates that it is indeed the true sheet that covered Jesus at his death. The carbon-14 age testing is still a controversy that has yet to be settled, but for now most scientists believe its findings until proven otherwise. The history of the Shroud is another area of controversy, however, as is the cloth itself and whether or not the image is indeed that of Christ. Let's explore these issues one by one.

I find it amazing that something as magnificent as this relic could have been kept from sight for so long—who had it, and why didn't word leak out that this priceless piece of Christianity was practically there for the taking? Cynics say that there's no history of the Shroud's origin, other than when it was first put on display in the 14th century; while believers claim that there *is* a history, which is now being brought forth. According to them, the Shroud is what early historians called the Edessa Cloth. This material was found in a wall in Edessa (in what is now Macedonia) in 544 and remained in the city until 944; next, it was moved to Constantinople, where it was found by crusaders sacking the city in 1204. It then disappeared until 1353—had it been hidden away?

The Edessa Cloth, also known as the Holy Mandylion, depicted a portrait of Jesus. Believers say that it was the Shroud of Turin folded up so that only his face was shown. And there's another piece of cloth known as the Sudarium of Oviedo, which is purportedly the cloth that covered the face of Jesus at his burial. Blood stains from the Sudarium link it with the Shroud of Turin, as forensic evidence shows the blood on the Sudarium to be of the same type (AB) as that on the Shroud. The Sudarium's history is not in question and has been dated to the time of Christ.

Also, botany and pollen experts Drs. Avinoam Danin and Uri Baruch have found pollen grains and flower images on the Shroud that are native to the Jerusalem area. In addition, other researchers state that the type of weave in the cloth is very similar to ones found in and around Jerusalem in the first century, particularly to fabric unearthed at the fortress of Masada. Others have found traces of dirt and limestone dust that is indigenous to Jerusalem and its environs on the Shroud.

Finally, while believers say that the Shroud of Turin is the burial cloth of Jesus, skeptics point out that even if it was found to be of first-century origin, what makes people think that the image on the cloth is that of Christ? They rightly point out that the image is only of a man with wounds that indicate a crucifixion, which, as my grandmother had pointed out, was the standard punishment for serious lawbreakers at the time of the Roman rule in the first century in Jerusalem. Doubters go on to state that the man could have been *any* criminal, not necessarily Jesus.

I think that when all is said and done, this becomes a matter of belief and faith . . . at least, I'd like it to be. I believe that the Shroud is a representation and not a true relic—but I don't think that should put a dent in our Christian belief. I have crosses all over my home and certainly don't believe that they're pieces of the actual structure that Jesus was crucified on, but, like the Shroud, my crosses remind me that Jesus walked the earth and died upon a cross, as so many did during Roman times.

I always remember what Grandma Ada used to say: The only thing we seem to remember about Jesus Christ is that he died an agonizing death. I have to agree—after all, what about the happy Christ, the teaching Christ, and the healing Christ? We only seem to recall the terrible sadness. (Many years after my grandmother passed, Francine told me that Jesus felt that his teachings fell short and all people remembered was his suffering and death.)

I believe that the Shroud of Turin was a painting (quite possibly done in blood) meant to portray Jesus' death. After all, Christ's Crucifixion was an event that inspired many works of art—but this particular creative person wanted to uniquely capture it on cloth.

Finally, I'd like to note that the Catholic Church has for the time being put a stop to any more investigations on carbon dating the Shroud, which I find very strange. If they felt it was authentic, why not open the doors to all investigations?

The belief still remains in the heart and mind of the beholder, so I feel that whatever gives you peace or reaffirms your knowledge, for God's sake (literally), go with it. As I stated before, it doesn't matter what I believe—if *you* think the Shroud is real, and it brings about spirituality or belief for you, then to each his own. I'm sure it will be a controversy that lasts for years, but as long as the Catholic Church puts up a block, nothing will ever be totally proven. Nevertheless, if we believe it to be, then it can be so.

26

The Holy Grail and the Holy Spirit

Historians and writers have hinted that a group of high-profile writers, scientists, and artists—including Walt Whitman, Victor Hugo, Arthur Conan Doyle, Isaac Newton, Sandro Botticelli, and the great Leonardo da Vinci—were not only reincarnationists, but also members of secret societies such as the sacred Priory of Sion, the Knights Templar, or the Masons.

In fact, not many people realize that along with being a great painter, Leonardo da Vinci was a prophet of sorts—not so much in written matter but in his sketches. I recommend that you check out his wondrous knowledge of technology and the structure of the human body: Long before science and medicine caught up to him, he'd made sketches of flying machines, helicopters, rockets, war machines, and cars; as well as finely detailed sketches of muscles, tendons, organs, and other body parts. He was way ahead of his time, and it wouldn't be until centuries later that much of what he drew would come to pass.

Leonardo also had knowledge of the Holy Grail, including where and what it was. The books *Holy Blood, Holy Grail* and *The Messianic Legacy* by Michael Baigent, Richard Leigh, and Henry Lincoln scratch the surface of this topic, but Dan Brown's novel *The Da Vinci Code* breaks it wide open. Most Gnostics (which my church is dedicated to) have known this "secret" information all along, but the Rosicrucians guarded it with a vengeance because the known world of Christianity would have branded this the worst of heresies.

So now with information about the Holy Grail coming out all over, we Gnostics feel a certain amount of exhilaration over a real truth of Christianity being brought forth. That's why long before *The Da Vinci Code* came out, I told my publisher that I wanted to write about Mother God and uncover Her once and for all—no matter how controversial it might be.

You see, the Crusaders knew that there wasn't really a grail (or cup as such) at all; instead, there was a *holder* of the sacred knowledge, which was the womb of mankind. Early Christians even went underground with this knowledge to avoid persecution by the Catholic Church. Some French libraries have much information on this subject, but after *Holy Blood, Holy Grail* was published, they shut their doors to more research. (It's also interesting to note that *The Da Vinci Code* takes place in France for the most part.)

So concerned was the paternal side of Christianity that they feigned ignorance on what da Vinci knew about the Grail, and many people were mysteriously killed because they possessed this knowledge. As God will have it, though, we can only keep truth buried for so long before Mother God will rise up and reestablish a kinder, gentler Christianity. It's now becoming quite apparent that there must be two sides.

If you've read my book *Mother God,* then you probably have a better handle on this long-buried, supposedly mysterious information that's been known since long before Christ's birth, but was suppressed by men who felt it took away from Christianity. How it would is beyond me—unless it just points to patriarchal control and the fact that these men would have had a hard time explaining what they've covered up for all these years.

Dan Brown also has another powerful book that addresses this topic, called *Angels & Demons.* And if you read the Dead Sea Scrolls in depth, you'll discover that Mary was known to channel information, another fact that seems to be hidden and only held by the Essenes (the forerunners of the Gnostics) . . . it's only a matter of time before the truth about the Mother Goddess—as well as the "Holy Grail"—becomes common knowledge.

The Holy Spirit

When I was in Catholic school and we made the sign of the cross, it was for the Father, the Son, and the Holy Ghost. Then, many people began to change *Ghost* to *Spirit* (I guess they felt that the words *Holy Ghost* smacked of being too esoteric).

Anyway, there has always been a controversy regarding the idea of three persons in one God. St. Patrick was supposed to have taken a shamrock (which we still see in Irish dishes, rings, and so on) to try to explain the Trinity, saying that it was three separate entities on one stem. It still seemed so confusing to me, until I came to understand that the third person in the Trinity was actually Mother God.

Some people believe that the Holy Spirit was the love between the Father and Mother that made the Son. Logically, this makes more sense when you see that the Church tried to obliterate the feminine principle. We have the Father, the Mother, and the Son, who came from the divinity of male God and female God. So the early Church decided to just name Mother God the "Holy Ghost."

The Holy Spirit's symbol of the dove came about because such a bird was seen over the head of Jesus. So from then on, the dove was used as a symbol of the Holy Spirit, which of course means peace, but doesn't have anything to do with Mother God.

I don't by any means think that you have to change your sign of the cross—I'm just giving you an insight into history and what your logical mind and heart will tell you.

27
The Lost Years of Jesus

This subject has elicited much debate and conjecture over the years. Yet in this chapter, I don't want to just tell you about the lost years of Jesus before he started his public life; I'd also like to give you information long known to our ministry, such as how Christ spent his days after he was crucified.

Jesus' Life from 12 to 30

The Bible depicts a 12-year-old Jesus helping his stepfather, Joseph—who, contrary to popular belief, was not a poor carpenter, but was instead a very wealthy custom-furniture maker. Indeed, both Mary and Joseph came from royal families—Joseph was, in fact, from the royal House of David—and they were highly esteemed in Judaic society. (To fast-forward to prove my point, why do you think Christ was invited into the best homes, and the wealthy such as Lazarus sought him out? Who paid for the Last Supper? And why was Jesus invited to wedding feasts? Certainly in Judaic society, lowly peasants were never welcome at such events. In addition, Christ's robes were of such fine cloth that when he was crucified, the Roman soldiers "cast lots" over them—in other words, they gambled to obtain his robes.)

The Bible then loses track of Jesus until he shows back up in Jerusalem at the age of 30. Many years ago, Francine said that Jesus had left because he didn't want to marry, and he wanted to study other cultures. She also pointed out that in the 1890s, a Russian journalist named Nicholas Notovitch was convinced that Christ traveled to, and possibly studied in, India.

A group of us quickly looked up Notovich's book *The Unknown Life of Jesus Christ,* which was heretofore unfamiliar to us, and found that it had been attacked and debunked numerous times by theologians and historians, and that Mr. Notovitch had been highly ostracized. (Hmm . . . does that sound familiar?)

In his book, Notovitch mentions a Tibetan text called *The Life of Saint Issa: Best of the Sons of Men,* which he heard about when he was a guest at a Buddhist monastery. According to this work, Christ left Jerusalem with a train of merchants when he was about 14, which was when most males were expected to marry, and he jour-neyed to India. (In my research, I've found comparable descriptions of these travels. Depending on the culture, Jesus is either called "Issa," "Isa," "Yuz Asaf," "Budasaf," "Yuz Asaph," "San Issa," or "Yesu.")

Notovitch was stunned by the parallel of "Issa's" teachings and martyrdom that coincided with Christ's life—and even his Crucifixion. The story of Saint Issa describes him arriving in India and settling among the Aryas, in the country "beloved by God."

Issa then went to Djagguernat (in the country of Orsis), where Brahman priests taught him to understand the Vedas, to cure physical ills by prayer, to teach sacred scriptures, and to drive out evil desires from man and make him in the likeness of God. For six years, Issa resided in other holy cities in India, living with and loving the lower classes, and siding with them against the oppressive upper classes.

Many writings, both recent and ancient, echo Notovitch's claim, as do the Aquarian Gospel and some of the Dead Sea Scrolls. *The Lost Years of Jesus* by Elizabeth Clare Prophet, *The Jesus Mystery* by Janet Brock, and *Jesus Lived In India* by Holger Kersten indicate that Christ was no stranger to the mystic East: He lived there, learned the ancient teachings, and returned to Palestine even more enlightened. Note that in Christ's teachings, even in his Beatitudes, there is a gentle Eastern flavor, so unlike the strict dogma of the Sanhedrin, which was the seat of the Judaic faith. He preached gentleness, caring, and paths of righteousness; along with bringing about a new order of love and a caring God, rather than a militant, hateful Creator who plays favorites.

Jesus then migrated from the Hindu faith to Buddhism. He mastered the Pali language and studied the sacred Buddhist scriptures, which enabled him to expound on sacred scrolls. Holger Kersten did a lot of research that corroborates information Francine told us many years ago: that Christ was also exposed to Buddhist teachings in Egypt. (We must remember that after his birth, Mary and Joseph did travel to that part of the Middle East with Jesus, and Francine says that they stayed there much longer than biblical records show.) Kersten said that most scholars acknowledge that Buddhist schools did in fact exist in Alexandria long before the time of Christ.

Jesus is also mentioned in the Persian historical work known as the *Rauzat-us-Safa,* written by Mir Muhammad Bin Khawand in A.D.1417:

> Jesus (on whom be peace) was named the "Messiah" because he was a great traveler. He wore a woolen scarf on his head and a woolen cloak on his body. He had a stick in his hand; he used to wander from country to country and from city to city. At nightfall he would stay where he was. He ate jungle vegetables, drank jungle water, and went on his travels on foot. His companions, in one of his travels, once bought a horse for him; he rode the horse one day, but as he could not make any provision for the feeding of the horse, he returned it. Journeying from his country, he arrived at Nasibain. With him were a few of his disciples whom he sent into the city to preach. In the city, however, there were current wrong and unfounded rumors about Jesus (on whom be peace) and his mother. The governor of the city, therefore, arrested the disciples and then summoned Jesus. Jesus miraculously healed some persons and exhibited other miracles. The king of the territory of Nasibain, therefore, with all his armies and his people, became a follower of his. The legend of the "coming down of food" contained in the Holy Qur'an belongs to the days of his travels.

The *Qisa Shazada Yuzasaph wo hakim Balauhar* (an Urdu version of the *Book of Balauhar and Budasaf*) tells of Christ (or Yuz

THE LOST YEARS OF JESUS

Asaf) preaching to the people of Kashmir and surrounding areas, asking people to come to the kingdom of God, which was not of this earth. Then we see him again in the book *Tarikh-i-Kashmir*, which was written by historian Mullah Nadri:

> During this time Hazrat Yuz Asaf having come from Bait-ul Muqaddas [the Holy Land] to this holy valley proclaimed his prophethood. He devoted himself, day and night, in [prayers to] God, and having attained the heights of piety and virtue, he declared himself to be a Messenger [of God] for the people of Kashmir.

Mullah also states clearly that Jesus was born in the Holy Land and proclaimed that he was a prophet of the children of Israel, or the Jewish people. He also states that Christ's beliefs were like those of the Hindus. (Of course they would be—we Gnostics seem to go above the dogma to the truth of a loving God that we can all identify with.)

In the book *A Search for the Historical Jesus* by Dr. Fida Hassnain, he cites a Tibetan manuscript that was translated from an ancient Chinese document called *The History of Religion and Doctrines: The Glass Mirror* that contained information about Jesus. The relevant portions are below:

> Yesu, the teacher and founder of the religion, who was born miraculously, proclaimed himself the Savior of the world. He commanded his disciples to observe the ten vows [Ten Commandments], among which includes prohibition of manslaughter and attainment of eternal joy through good deeds. . . . This is one of the virtuous results emerging out of the teachings of the Buddha. His doctrines did not spread extensively, but

survived in Asia for a long period. The above information is derived from the Chinese treatises on religions and doctrines.

In addition, Jesus is noted in Kashmir in the Buddhist *Book of Balauhar and Budasaf;* the *Ikmal-ud-Din,* authored by scholar Al-Shaikh Al-Said-us-Sadiq (who died in 962), who traveled many countries to research his book, also speaks of Christ's travels to Kashmir, including his death in that country of natural causes at the age of 120 (but as we'll see, he actually died in France).

Perhaps the most interesting text relating to Christ's time in this country is an official decree of the Grand Mufti of Kashmir issued in 1774. Jesus is even referred to on a signpost outside his purported burial site of Roza Bal, and there's also a mention of him at the Takhat Sulaiman (Throne of Solomon) monument in Srinagar. There are four inscriptions on this monument, two of which are still legible. The inscriptions were recorded, however, and read as follows:

1. The mason of this pillar is Bihishti Zargar. Year fifty and four.

2. Khwaja Rukun son of Murjan erected this pillar.

3. At this time Yuz Asaf proclaimed his prophethood. Year fifty and four.

4. He is Jesus, Prophet of the Children of Israel.

So we see that not only did Jesus visit many different countries, as Francine said, but he also taught long before the Bible

stated. I'm sure that he was received in these foreign lands better than he was in Jerusalem and Bethlehem. I feel that Jesus was more at peace in these Eastern locales, not only because he'd learned so much, but also because he could move freely without fear of condemnation.

In fact, there are at least 30 ancient texts covering the main religions of Hinduism, Buddhism, and Islam that very specifically mention Jesus—not only before his public life and Crucifixion, but also afterward, when he continued to perform his ministry in the Middle East and India.

Now, these ancient texts haven't been ignored by scholars, who put forth theories about the lost years of Jesus and his living after the Crucifixion, but they *have* been suppressed by many Christian scholars and certainly by the Catholic Church. Why? You know the answer as well as I: They didn't want information leaking out that could perhaps mar Christianity, as it's been put forth for centuries by the patriarchal powers that be.

Putting religion aside for a moment, let's get logical: If all these references to Jesus were pure fiction, then why did so many writers from various religious backgrounds talk about this wonderful prophet and messiah—I mean, for what reason would they make up a fictional character? It doesn't make sense. . . . These writers were historians, theologians, and eyewitnesses to Christ and his mission in the East and the many teachings that he gave. So is there a massive cover-up here?

Christian scholars know that *many* Gospels were written— not just the four officially recognized ones of Mark, Matthew, Luke, and John. These Gospels date from about A.D. 70 to the second century, while the "synoptic" Gospels—Mark, Matthew, and Luke—are very similar and come from a common source.

John's is inherently different, in that it names people and two episodes (the wedding at Cana and the raising of Lazarus) not mentioned in the other Gospels, and it's also newer.

So why were these other books not included in the Bible? Well, they were too controversial, in that many of them conflicted with the "four true Gospels" and the Church's idea of what Christianity should be. (Of note here is that modern Christianity is more or less based on Paul's understanding of Jesus and his message. Yet, ironically, Paul never even knew Jesus. But then Paul was a Roman citizen and proud of it, and his thinking was more in line with what early Rome and Christianity wanted.)

I'm not going to point out every single text that mentions Christ teaching in their area, but you can certainly research the books I've mentioned to find more information. It's so wonderful that all this truth is coming out (along with the Dead Sea Scrolls, which Francine says Christ *did* help write), and that we can research what's been long buried but secretly known by many, without fear of being branded heretics or burned at some stake.

Before I go on, I'd like to share how thrilled I am, and have always been, that not only was Christ an educated student, but being a true Gnostic, he genuinely did what he told us all to do: seek and find. Even though the Gnostics and Essenes have been around since before the advent of Christianity, they were stuck for more knowledge, and after his travels, Jesus came back and filled in the blanks, as it were.

If you look at the Gnostic Gospels, you'll find glaring comparisons to Judaism, Christianity (that is, Christ's own infusions), Hinduism, and Buddhism. So I guess we can rightfully say that being a true Gnostic, Jesus incorporated it all into what we still

say today—he had a bottom-line philosophy of a loving God and doing good.

Don't you find it enormously comforting—and doesn't it give you great pride—to know that so many cultures embraced Jesus as either a messiah (messenger) or prophet from God when they were of different races, cultures, and religions? It also gives you pause to realize that it wasn't just the apostles who spread the word of this direct report from God—others also recognized Christ's divinity and teachings without any hesitation. It really gives a new and truer meaning to what Jesus once said: "Only in his hometown and in his own house is a prophet without honor" (Matthew 13:57).

When Jesus *did* return to teach in the synagogue in his hometown, many were amazed, wondering, "What's this wisdom that has been given him that he even does miracles? Isn't this the carpenter? Isn't this Mary's son and the brother of James, Joseph, Judas, and Simon? Aren't his sisters here with us?" (Mark 6:2–3, Matthew 13:53–58). They were shocked that Jesus, their hometown boy, had such wisdom and could teach with power and work miracles.

Now, two things jump out to the logical mind: Christ was, of course, endowed by God, and not just spiritually—he also had a tremendous healing ability; and he came from a family that was wealthy enough to be able to send him to school to read. He also must have gained, as we all do who travel or study, a great deal of theological knowledge as time went on. When I go to Turkey, Greece, Egypt, France, Germany, Ireland, and so on, one of the first things I do is to talk to scribes, archaeologists, and the locals because they know their cultures so well.

———·•◄∞►•·———

Francine says that the time Jesus spent in India were the best years of his life. He formed a group of disciples who followed him, and he met Mary Magdalene, who was absolutely not a harlot—although the Church's teachings have tried to make her out as such because they didn't know what else to do with her. To erase her from his life was almost impossible because she was always around, but if they made her a sinner who just tagged along for the ride (so to speak), then she couldn't be a threat.

Mary Magdalene was actually a very high-born woman espoused to a centurion. Magdalene didn't know the man was married until his wife wanted her stoned, which was the punishment of the day for adultery. Christ heard about this and came to her aid, not only protecting her, but telling the true story of how the centurion had tricked Mary Magdalene. Her gratitude made her love him . . . and he was already sure he was in love with her. They were married not long after that in a secret ceremony.

When Jesus was 29, he and Mary Magdalene returned to Israel. There, as we know, he preached ethical standards through his parables about everything from how to treat one's slaves and neighbors to how to handle one's money and family matters, along with how humankind could reach spiritual perfection.

Jesus' Belief in Reincarnation

While we're delving into the mystery of the lost years of Jesus, I'd like to not only discuss his private life, but also touch on some of the beliefs that were left out of the Bible, one of which is reincarnation. It's long been bandied about by theologians, but there's much proof, and not just in the Dead Sea Scrolls, that the Essenes or Gnostics were reincarnationists—and certainly if Christ studied the Vedas and Buddhism, he would have embraced the philosophy.

Francine states that when Constantine wanted everyone converted to Christianity, all the books that contained references to reincarnation were destroyed. The remnants that survived were then edited out by the early Catholic Church. (As an aside, I don't logically understand how believing in many lifetimes distorts or negates Christianity—if anything, it enhances the greatness and goodness of God that Christ tried to convey. To give humankind many chances to advance through lessons is much more reasonable and just than one life in which we could be born deformed, poor, rich, or any number of experiences. It makes God an equal-opportunity employer and creator.)

About 35 years ago, Francine told me that Jesus was a great believer in reincarnation. We know that the people of India believe in it, and there have been many cases even recently in which we hear of children giving detailed accounts of past lives. The data supporting reincarnation has been accumulating at an increasing rate by learned Ph.D.'s, psychiatrists, and M.D.'s, using (as we in my church do) past-life regression as a powerful healing tool. I can personally attest to hundreds of accounts of children and adults relating precise details of other lives.

Scholars have looked at the Gospels for clues that Jesus actually taught reincarnation, although most of these writings were either destroyed, banned, or edited by the Church. However, let's examine Matthew 11:14: "And if you are willing to accept it, he [John the Baptist] is Elijah who was to come." In Matthew

17:10–13, Jesus again relates that Elijah came but wasn't known, for he was John the Baptist.

The only logical implication is that Jesus is talking of Elijah having been a past life of John the Baptist, who would be reborn again sometime in the future. Another interesting observation is that whenever Christ talked about the body, he used the metaphor of a structure or edifice, always referring to the body as a temple. The analogy would hold true that when he speaks of his Father's house having many mansions, it suggests that we can occupy many temples or bodies.

Another clue is found in Matthew 16:13–15: "When Jesus came into the quarters of Cesarea Philippi, he asked his disciples, 'Who do people say that the Son of Man is?' They replied, 'Some John the Baptist; others say Elijah; and still others Jeremiah or one of the prophets.' 'But what about you?' he asked." Why would Jesus even bring this up, unless he believed in the whole premise of life after life? This would also bear out what the Essenes or Gnostics believed, as well as Christ's study in the East, where most of the Eastern religions believe in reincarnation. He would have accepted and even taught this doctrine.

After the Crucifixion

Now let's get into what is probably the most controversial part of Christ's life: whether or not he survived the Crucifixion. Even though some of the material here has been subject to great debate, there are many writings that support Nicholas Notovitch's theories of Jesus living in India. We'll also see that we run into

the same conflicts about Christ's Crucifixion and death—or in this case, his *survival* of death.

Most of the so-called secret societies—which are not so secret anymore, thanks to the books *Holy Blood, Holy Grail* and *The Messianic Legacy* by Michael Baignet; the recent *The Da Vinci Code* by Dan Brown; and Elaine Pagels's volumes on the Dead Sea Scrolls—believe that Christ did not die on the cross. Even the Acta Thomae (Acts of Thomas), which was banned as heretical in 495 by a decree of Gelasius, say that Christ was with Thomas at a wedding in A.D. 49, a full 16 years after the Crucifixion!

Francine gave out this information almost 30 years ago, before it had become a serious subject for study. It was never secret, as anyone who came into our Gnostic services or classes will attest to. Instead of being hush-hush about it, we've openly discussed it in our sermons for many years. And Pope John XXIII, who was my hero, once said something very telling: that Christian belief should not be based on the fact that Christ died on the cross.

There's too much evidence surfacing now to just sweep under the rug, so why was it perpetuated that he died? Well, one of the reasons is guilt: "He died for our sins." But why? Each person is responsible for his or her own chart and to live a good life as Christ taught—so why would Jesus have to take on *our* chart?

Francine states that there's no doubt that Jesus was put on trial, humiliated, beaten, and made to carry his cross at least part of the way. Indeed, he *was* put up on the cross—but the interesting thing to note is that, unlike all the other crucified people of the time, Jesus' legs strangely weren't broken. He was also given a footrest, which would have allowed him to push himself up to breathe, thereby prolonging death.

She goes on to say that Pontius Pilate, who was vilified in writings and documents aside from Biblical texts, was in on the conspiracy to let Christ hang for three hours and appear to be dead—after which, Pilate had Jesus taken down. And he made sure that the time of the Crucifixion was such that Christ would only be on the cross for a short period of time due to the honoring of the Sabbath. This satisfied the detractors at the time, and gave new meaning to Pontius Pilate "washing his hands of this innocent man."

Francine told me that Jesus was given an opiate-like drug that made him go into a deep swoon, which simulated death. In 1982, Professor J. D. M. Derrett theorized that Jesus was crucified but either lapsed into unconsciousness or put himself in a self-induced trance (quite possible when he studied in India and the East); being taken for dead, he was then removed from the cross.

The scholar Karl Friedrich Bahrdt (1741–1792) postulated that Jesus survived a feigned death with Luke the physician having supplied drugs to him beforehand (which supports what Francine said). Friedrich also said that Jesus was an Essene (which is the same as an early Gnostic), as was Joseph of Arimathea, who resuscitated him. No one seems to question the fact that this rich man (Joseph) just offered his tomb to Christ out of the blue. Of course he did—because it was set up beforehand that Jesus would be resuscitated.

Again, underlying this and other hypotheses about Christ's survival is the fact that, as Francine says, death on the cross was always designed to be painful and long in coming (usually up to several days). When Jesus was taken down from the cross—without his legs being broken—relatively early on the same day, Josephus (the Jewish historian) wrote that he'd seen other prisoners crucified, and after several days, they still hadn't died—even though they'd had their legs broken.

Now, Jesus certainly did appear to Mary and Mary Magdalene and all the apostles—a ghost would hardly be able to tell Thomas ("Doubting Thomas") to feel his wounds. I know a lot about ghosts, and trust me, you can't touch them, nor do they have wounds. When Mary and Mary Magdalene came to the tomb and saw the angels, the angels asked: "Why do you look for the living among the dead?" (Luke 24:5).

Later Jesus appeared to his apostles to prove that he was still alive, saying, "Peace be with you. . . . Why are you troubled, and why do thoughts arise in your hearts? See my hands and feet, that it is I myself! Touch and see, for a ghost doesn't have flesh and bones, as you see me to have." Then he showed them his hands and feet. Next, he asked, "Do you have anything here to eat?" And they offered him a piece of a broiled fish, and he ate it in their presence (Luke 24:36–43).

I don't know about you, but I've never known a ghost or a spirit to need food. The reason Jesus did this was to show everyone that he was alive, and that even a God-man needed to eat food. Aside from his attempts to assure everyone that they weren't seeing an apparition, Jesus was extremely hungry after having gone through pure hell.

However, this appearance, along with the empty tomb on Easter morning, has provided ample fuel for scholars and theologians to explore Christ's survival of the Crucifixion. The incentive has been furthered by the fact that there is a complete lack of documentation concerning the Resurrection—except for Paul's account (who, as stated earlier, never met Jesus). Even though the early Christian church seemed to perpetuate the story of Christ's death, the countless documents from so many countries that support his survival, travel, and teachings warranted investigation.

None of this, by any means, negates the fact that Jesus was a supernatural being; it just means that he appeared to say good-bye to his disciples and, just like the Bible states, to give them instructions to go out and teach his words. He must have felt that he could do more good by teaching in another country than by staying home—where he'd certainly be hounded, and might even really be killed, for spreading his great message of love and a loving God.

More clues of Christ's surviving the Crucifixion show up in texts that were written by the apostles but not officially accepted by the Church or included in the Bible, as well as in books that were banned or destroyed at the time of the Bible's compilation. (The Dead Sea Scrolls and the Nag Hammadi were discovered much later.) For example, the Acts of Thomas explain that before Christ left, he met with Thomas several times after the Crucifixion. Francine says that's when Jesus dictated his last messages of love, hope, and knowledge; this also explains how Christ sent Thomas to spread his spirituality teachings throughout India, possibly because he knew he'd be safe.

It's in Anatolia (the part of Turkey that comprises the peninsula of Asia Minor) that Christ met with Thomas again. Jesus and the two Marys had moved along the west coast of Turkey. I can certainly bear this out firsthand from being in that country—Turkish people talk about Jesus' being there freely, and with such truth, knowledge, and belief. There is also proof of his being in Turkey at an old stopping place for travelers called "The Home of Mary," found along the ancient silk route. From here, Christ could easily have entered Europe and France.

Francine says that Jesus, Mary, and Mary Magdalene criss-crossed into Turkey and then went east to India and Kashmir again before finally coming back through Italy and eventually settling in France. (It's no coincidence that many books such as *Holy Blood, Holy Grail*, as well as the uncovered texts of the "secret" early Christian societies, take place in France.) After suffering the scorn and mockery of his own people as well as the Romans, Christ decided that he'd be better off teaching in another area. So he went on to teach for some years in the East before he came to stay in France.

Francine says that Jesus and Mary Magdalene settled around the Rennes-le-Château area of France, had seven children together, and lived into their late 80s. Thus, the Knights Templar and the secret societies of the Rosy Cross and the Priory of Sion—and even parts of the early Masons—were set up to protect Christ, Mary Magdalene, and their bloodline.

Now, you need to make up your own mind here, but as I stated before, paraphrasing Pope John XXIII, why do Christians need to believe that Jesus died on the cross? I can't say enough that no one has to believe anything except what feels like truth to him or her. I pray that you keep an open mind and research, read, and let your heart stay open.

We as Gnostics follow Christ's teachings to the letter, but we also know that there is so much more that he left behind that isn't generally known. That he left those teachings with others who follow the Hindu, Buddhist, and Islamic faiths just enhances his message of bringing love and peace to the world. He did survive against all adversity by following his own example—and so can we.

When you do uncover the truth, it makes your soul soar, and even increases your love and admiration fo Christ . . . but it also opens the door to criticism and controversy. I often wonder why—I mean, when something enhances and betters, as truth and knowledge always do, does it threaten those who have lived in a box of ignorance? I've always felt, as have many of my ministers (who, I'd like to proudly add, are scholars in their own right), that this information gave us a deeper knowledge, more purpose, and a more profound love of Christ than we ever had, and it made us want to follow his ways more then we ever did before.

Even today, to preach love and goodness is too simple—it flies in the face of both Christian and Jewish dogma. It also upsets the political structure of the Church *and* the millions upon millions of dollars that its members tithe to build big cathedrals and such. (Amazing, isn't it, especially when Christ taught in a field or on a mountainside.)

Do I believe in building structures to honor God? You bet I do. But I don't want to see some obnoxious house of worship; instead, I'd like a home for children and the elderly, and hospices for the sick. That's how we can glorify God in the long term . . . not just for an hour every Sunday.

We can be defamed and even crucified by life, but like Jesus, we can leave behind a better world through the good deeds we do. In other words, we can live our life as Christlike as we can, with a gentle persuasion. Jesus studied, and so should we—and we should ultimately bear witness to what he said by living an exemplary life.

28
The Devil

I briefly talked about this subject in another book, but I'll go deeper into it here: The greatest tulpa ever perpetuated is good ol' Lucifer, or Beelzebub, or whatever name the culture deems to give to this "fallen angel."

Angels and prophets—even parties, family life, and the planting of grain—are mentioned more in the Bible than any devil, yet humankind has dogmatically made one of them bigger than life. The devil has gained so much popularity that one could wonder if we don't, in some circles, occupy ourselves more with him than we do with Christ or God.

The devil starts out in the Bible as a snake that convinces Eve to urge Adam to eat the forbidden fruit of the tree of knowledge, and then he intermittently reappears whenever there's a plague. He turns up next in the book of Job—which I recommend that everyone read—when he and God are speaking to each other. As adversarial as it may seem, there's no damnation. God more or less tells the devil that he can do anything but kill Job, which is a test of Job's faith in God. It's also a good analogy for every one of us whenever we're tempted to choose evil over good, especially when we're faced with the loss of everything, as Job was.

As for Jesus, one of the only times he addresses the devil directly is when he tells the devil to get behind him, almost as we do when we put bad thoughts behind us. Also, when Jesus is in the desert, the devil takes him to the top of a mountain and tells him that if he accepts the devil (evil and power), all that he surveys will be his. Our Lord, of course, declines. Now, isn't this as true today as it was then—that if we succumb to absolute power, our soul is in jeopardy of succumbing to pure materialism, to the point that no light from spirituality can penetrate?

Of course, I believe that evil abounds in darkness and dark entities, but I don't believe in giving this one singular tulpa so much power. Instead, I prefer to give *God* the power of my love and devotion.

Regardless of what you believe, I can't repeat it enough: Use your own logical mind here!

29
The Mythology of Popular Holidays

I thought I'd end the book on a somewhat lighter, more festive note, by looking at a few of our holidays . . . which are actually ancient rituals whose history has gotten lost in the chronicles of time.

Halloween

The word *Halloween* comes from All Hallows' Eve, a Christian celebration that takes place the night before All Saints' Day. Yet the holiday has ancient pagan roots, and today it's also a high holy day for Wicca, the beautiful nature-oriented and ancient religion dominated by white witches.

However, just as with many of our holidays that have their feet firmly planted in pagan tradition, the Church took over—possibly as a case of "If you can't beat 'em, join 'em." It's very much like Mardi Gras, which is observed in various parts of the world, especially in Rio de Janeiro and New Orleans. Many who party with abandon both physically and mentally don't even know why they're celebrating—they don't realize that Mardi Gras honors the oncoming period of Lent, in which people are piously supposed to give up earthly pleasures as a sacrifice for the 40 days leading up to the anniversary of the Last Supper of Jesus.

Traditionally, the ancient Celtic end-of-summer harvest festival, called Samhain (usually pronounced *SOW-en*), also took place on November 1. It was believed that on this day, the world of the gods would be visible to humans. Since this was a time when the souls of the dead were believed to visit homes and leave messages in dreams, many fortune-tellers felt that it was the best time to predict future events.

Druids recognized this festival as being interrelated with the harvest, the full moon, and astrological changes. Then, after conquering Britain, the Romans added these Celtic traditions to their own harvest festival, Cerelia, which was celebrated on October 4.

As a result, some traditions were changed, while others survived—such as the belief in ghosts and witches. And my spirit guide Francine says that the tradition of leaving food out for the dead came about because ancient people felt that ghosts might be hungry after a year of being deprived, but if they were given food, the spirits would leave everyone alone. Thus, "trick or treat" was born.

Other traditions include:

- **Dunking for apples,** which wasn't just a game—
  Francine says that it was all rooted, as so many of
  our rituals are, in good fortune. The more apples
  you could get, the better your luck would be during the following year; if a maiden was able to snag
  an apple, she was sure to be married within a year.

- **Bonfires** were set in the hopes that the sun would
  come out and stay for longer periods of time so that
  the harvest would yield more crops. The bonfires
  also attracted mosquitoes, which in turn attracted
  owls and bats—who were therefore incorporated in
  the whole All Hallow's Eve mythology. (Francine
  also says that the lighting of fires or bonfires came
  about as a way to ward off evil spirits.)

- Bonfires were also supposed to encourage fairies
  to come out of their mounds and walk among us,
  and many believed that's why we **dress up:** to
  become something we're not. Donning costumes
  and masks was also believed to confuse or frighten
  away evil spirits.

- The Irish and Scottish are responsible for the
  tradition of carving **jack-o-lanterns,** which was
  part of their harvest celebration. Originally, they
  carved faces in turnips and potatoes, but when

they emigrated to America, they began carving pumpkins as well.

The lighting of a candle in the jack-o-lantern is the same as the Druids lighting fires; it also showed the souls of the departed where to go, and was a protection against evil spirits as well. (Note that even when the sun is out in the middle of the day, there are still candles lit in a church. I think this has just become tradition—it's not necessarily acknowledgment of the fact that spirits can see burning energy such as a candle better than artificial light.)

- Halloween was believed to be the easiest time to **contact the dead** because the veil was supposedly at its thinnest. There are still people who want me to conduct a trance for them on Halloween, as if that's the only day our loved ones are available!

Here's a bit of trivia: Judas was considered the 13th person at the Last Supper, which is why 13 is supposed to be a doomed or unlucky number. Even though no one really knows who was actually present at the Last Supper, the number 13 is still considered unlucky—some modern-day buildings don't even have 13th floors! (Take a look the next time you're staying at a hotel.)

It's just like the number 666, which is supposed to be the devil's number—when, in actuality, most archaeologists, and even a few theologians (and Francine), have validated that the number was the address of Nero, the Roman emperor who burned Rome and blamed it on the Christians. It makes sense because

Nero certainly was an insane, devilish person, but to just assign a number to the devil is really ludicrous—especially when the Bible didn't fully come together until the early fourth century.

The number 666 was subsequently put forth in the Book of Revelation as a record of the vision of a man named John. This book was made part of the Bible, and has influenced millions to believe in an Antichrist and a battle called Armageddon, which, in turn, flies in the face of the all-loving and merciful God that Christ tried to put forth. It just goes to show that some organized religions—and ultimately, some of humankind—seem to need to focus on fear, demons, and devils, instead of love, peace, and goodwill.

Other Holidays

Our world is filled with pagan symbols—take, for example, the wedding band. It was believed that if bad luck came to a married couple, it would get trapped in a circle (the ring), and it would just stay there, running in a circle for eternity.

Pagan influence can also be clearly seen in the following holidays.

Christmas

In Dan Brown's *The Da Vinci Code*, one of the main characters points out that December 25 was the birthday of the pre-Christian god Mithras, who was called "the son of God and the Light of the World" . . . and he was supposedly buried in a rock tomb and resurrected three days later. December 25 was also the birthday of Osiris, Adonis, and Dionysus—all pagan gods.

The Christmas tree is a definite pagan symbol as well. Trees, in the ancient beliefs, carried the devas of Lilith, the queen of the underworld. To bring a tree into your home meant that you brought in good luck from the fairies. To this day, when we want to attract good fortune, we still knock on wood, which some say is derived from the following greeting: "Are you listening, Lilith, to my wish that nothing bad happens?"

It's a shame that Christmas has become such a commercial overindulgence, synonymous with spending as much money as possible. The real spiritual meaning and accompanying festivities are sadly becoming a faint memory. Grandma Ada, who was born in 1865 to a very wealthy family in Germany, told me that her kin used to celebrate Christmas with oranges (which were very hard to get then); after which, the family would have all their friends and relatives over to sing Christmas carols, play games, and eat. Whenever I think about it, I'm saddened when I compare this to how we "celebrate" the birth of Christ today.

Easter

In ancient times, Easter had nothing to do with Christ's Resurrection—instead, it was venerated as the coming of spring, flowers, and the planting season. The Easter bunny was added later as a nod to the rabbit's prolific mating habits.

The egg, long a symbol of birth, wormed its way into Easter as well. (I guess the pagans were just trying to cover all their bases.) Sure, fertility may be important now, but you must remember that it was the lifeline of these ancient peoples: Not only did it keep the bloodlines alive, but it also ensured that there'd be more children in the fields to harvest crops so that people could eat and, therefore, survive.

Thanksgiving

Thanksgiving, of course, started with the Pilgrims . . . yet there might not have been any turkey at the first feast. (Corn, vegetables, fowl, venison, and fish were believed to have been enjoyed instead.) Regardless, just like the bunny and the egg, the turkey (bird) is another symbol of fertility, which was revered far back into antiquity—even the Egyptians had gods such as Horus and Thoth, who had bird heads. The bird also seems to represent freedom, just like the dove in Christianity denotes peace, hope, and many times the Holy Spirit.

On Halloween, when little witches or tiny ghosts trick-or-treat at my door, I'll be standing there with a bowl of candy thinking about all the Druids who fought so hard to keep this a sacred day. And the next time you look at your Christmas tree, hold a bunny, or see an egg, I hope you'll take a moment to remember all those who went before us and gave us these rituals we enjoy today.

Sadly, we criticize the so-called pagans for their beliefs, yet we have no problem cannibalizing their high holy days or rituals and making them our own.

Afterword

We've barely scratched the surface of the world's secrets in this book; nevertheless, I've attempted to shed some light on the mysteries that have been most often talked about, as well as debated. I can only tell you that, from years of research and using my psychic abilities, these are my findings. Whether you agree or not is totally up to you. As I've always said, "Take with you what you want and leave the rest"—but like me, I hope that you'll research and read on your own. After all, as the main character says in *Auntie Mame*, "Life is a banquet!"

Never quit searching and exploring because therein lies our heritage—and, at the bottom of it all, we discover humankind's search for ourselves and especially our search for God. Just remember that all answers are there for the asking, and under God's time, here or when we go to the Other Side, all will be researched—and so much will be revealed.

It's amazing that we look so hard for answers. With all the enigmas in the world, God is always in our heart and all around us . . . and that's no mystery.

God love you, I do . . .
Sylvia

Acknowledgments

I'd like to thank the people who put all their time and energy into researching this material. There are so many mysteries still unsolved, but without these people giving their time to scientific research, and encouraging others to look outside their narrow existence, a whole world that carries more mysteries than we'd ever have enough lifetimes to explore would be closed to us forever.

The Internet puts a wealth of knowledge about these subjects at your fingertips, but the ones I've covered here also can be researched in any number of books. I always suggest that you educate yourself, for it makes your vista of knowledge greater, and it certainly makes you a more interesting person, as you help your mind expand itself out of its tiny world.

235

About the Author

Sylvia Browne is the #1 *New York Times* best-selling author and world-famous psychic medium who appears regularly on the *Montel Williams Show* and *Larry King Live*, as well as making countless other media and public appearances. With her down-to-earth personality and great sense of humor, Sylvia thrills audiences on her lecture tours—and she's still found the time to write nine immensely popular books (so far). Holding a master's degree in English literature, Sylvia lives in California and plans to write as long as she can hold a pen.

Please contact Sylvia at: **www.sylvia.org**, or call **(408) 379-7070** for further information about her work.

About the Artist

Kirk Simonds is a fantasy illustrator and artist whose mother and sister are in Sylvia's ministry. He's very proud of the work that they do and of the ministry, which tries to promote the truth, logic, and compassion behind beliefs and spirituality. He was honored to be asked by Sylvia to illustrate her concepts on the unexplained and mysterious.

Hay House Titles of Related Interest

After Life, by John Edward

Angel Medicine, by Doreen Virtue, Ph.D.

Diary of a Psychic, by Sonia Choquette

The God Code, by Gregg Braden

Healing with the Fairies, by Doreen Virtue, Ph.D.

Psychic Navigator, by John Holland (book-with-CD)

Sacred Ceremony, by Steven D. Farmer, Ph.D.

Secrets & Mysteries, by Denise Linn

Spirit Messenger, by Gordon Smith

The Ultimate Astrologer, Nicholas Campion

You Can Heal Your Life, by Louise L. Hay

All of the above are available at your local bookstore, or may be
ordered by visiting: Hay House USA: **www.hayhouse.com**
Hay House Australia: **www.hayhouse.com.au**
Hay House UK: **www.hayhouse.co.uk**
Hay House South Africa: **orders@psdprom.co.za**

We hope you enjoyed this Hay House book.
If you would like to receive a free catalog featuring additional
Hay House books and products, or if you would like information about the
Hay Foundation, please contact:

Hay House, Inc.
P.O. Box 5100
Carlsbad, CA 92018-5100

(760) 431-7695 or (800) 654-5126
(760) 431-6948 (fax) or (800) 650-5115 (fax)
www.hayhouse.com

Published and distributed in Australia by:
Hay House Australia Pty. Ltd. • 18/36 Ralph St. • Alexandria NSW
2015 • *Phone:* 612-9669-4299 • *Fax:* 612-9669-4144
www.hayhouse.com.au

Published and distributed in the United Kingdom by:
Hay House UK, Ltd. • Unit 62, Canalot Studios
222 Kensal Rd., London W10 5BN • *Phone:* 44-20-8962-1230
Fax: 44-20-8962-1239 • www.hayhouse.co.uk

Published and distributed in the Republic of South Africa by:
Hay House SA (Pty), Ltd., P.O. Box 990, Witkoppen 2068
Phone/Fax: 2711-7012233 • orders@psdprom.co.za

Distributed in Canada by:
Raincoast • 9050 Shaughnessy St., Vancouver, B.C. V6P 6E5
Phone: (604) 323-7100 • *Fax:* (604) 323-2600

Sign up via the Hay House USA Website to receive the Hay House online
newsletter and stay informed about what's going on with your favorite authors.
You'll receive bimonthly announcements about: Discounts and Offers, Special
Events, Product Highlights, Free Excerpts, Giveaways, and more!
www.hayhouse.com

THIS IS THE NEWSLETTER YOU'VE BEEN WAITING FOR . . .

Find out
SYLVIA BROWNE'S
secrets for developing
your psychic powers!

Exclusive
SYLVIA BROWNE
Lecture Tape—FREE!

With one-year
subscription

Fold along dotted line.